IN EASY STAGES

Sonia Buist
&
Emily Keller

LOLITS Press
Portland, Oregon

Library of Congress Catalog Number 97-072120
International Standard Book Number 0-9643836-1-6

Writer and Editor - Sonia Buist
Illustrations and Cover - Emily Keller
Consultant - Judith Rose
Maps and Page Layout - Jeff Danforth
Elevation Charts - Emma Yuting Danforth
Printing - Paramount Graphics, Portland, Oregon
Bindery - Lincoln & Allen, Portland, Oregon

LOLITS is an acronym for **L**ittle **O**ld **L**adies **i**n
Tennis **S**hoes

Copies of *Around Mt Hood in Easy Stages* can be
ordered from

LOLITS Press
9840 SW Imperial Drive
Portland, OR 97225
(503) 292-0237
Fax (503) 292-2469

By the same authors, *Hikes & Walks on Mt Hood:
Government Camp and Timberline Lodge Areas,*
also available from LOLITS Press

TABLE OF CONTENTS

ACKNOWLEDGMENTS

We would like to acknowledge the help and support we got for this project from our families and friends. We would also like to acknowledge the contributions of Bruce Haynes, Pete Martin, and Terry Sroufe of the US Forest Service, who provided invaluable advice, Susan Sack who helped with the proofreading, and Mary Durham, who helped with the proofreading and wrote the chapter "Backpacking the Timberline Trail". The Oregon Historical Society kindly gave permission for the reproduction of the photograph on page 57 of the Summit of Mt Hood, 1896 (Zenus Moody Family, #OrHi 37884).

Many friends helped by testing out our instructions and maps. We are indebted to them for their comments and suggestions. We are happy to say that they all came back safely! The roll of honor includes:

Zach Bates
Cecille & Gary Beyle
Rose Bond
Lisa Brenner
Catriona & Diana Buist
Bob & Carol Carson
Andrea Davis
Mary Durham
Jim Gilmore
Alisa Fairweather
Steve Hall & Caroline Enns
Arthur Hayward
Liz Hunnicutt
Jim Honeycutt

Paul Keller
Jim Morris
Deanna Mueller Crispin
Molly Osborne
Lynn Oveson
Patricia Reilly
Matt Rizzo
Aaron Diaz Spencer
Tom & Martin Stibolt
David & Jane Turville
Adam, Jean & Bill Vollmer
Sandra Wilson
Carolyn Wood

INTRODUCTION & HOW TO USE THIS BOOK

The Timberline Trail is one of the most spectacular hiking trails in the world. The 40.7-mile trail circles Mt Hood, mostly at about the timber line level, and drops into and climbs out of canyons carved by the rivers that flow from the many glaciers on the mountain. Over the 40.7 miles of the trail, the total elevation gain is approximately 9000 ft., with the low point being 3200 ft. and the high point being 7560 ft. Most of the trail is in the Mt Hood Wilderness Area. The only developed areas are the two ski areas that the trail crosses, Timberline and Mt Hood Meadows.

Our purpose in writing this book is to show how the Timberline Trail can readily be broken down into one-way day hikes if you use a car shuttle or car swap. Two of the segments also offer the possibility of turning the hike into a loop so a shuttle or car swap is not needed. We have divided the 40.7 -mile circle into eight segments and describe how to reach the trailheads and trails that will provide access to the Timberline Trail. The access trails vary in length from less than a mile to three miles, and vary considerably in altitude gain. Two additional access trails, Pinnacle Ridge and Elk Cove Trails, are included to provide alternative access trails on the north side.

Each segment can be hiked either clockwise or counterclockwise. We use the terms *clockwise* and *counterclockwise* to describe the direction of the segment that is on the Timberline Trail, thinking of the entire trail loop as a circle. For example, to hike Segment One *clockwise*, start at Timberline Lodge and hike to the Ramona Falls Trailhead. To hike this segment *counterclockwise*, start at the Ramona Falls Trailhead and hike to Timberline Lodge (see p.12).

All of the segments of the Timberline Trail offer spectacular views, alpine meadows carpeted with wildflowers, beautiful streams lined with flowers, and quiet forests. Several offer the challenge of a river crossing.

We wanted to make this a book that tucks comfortably into a pocket. This imposed constraints on the amount of text we could include and on the size of maps. Our overriding aim was to be precise and accurate. We hope we have struck a balance that works for most people. For those who prefer to backpack around, we have included a section that describes what to take and where to camp.

HOW HIKES ARE CATEGORIZED

We have tried to provide guidance as to the relative difficulty of the trails, and the noteworthy features of each hike. To rank the trails by difficulty, we have taken into account the length, elevation gain, smoothness of the trail, and the altitude of the segment. The categories we have used are Moderately Strenuous, Strenuous, and Very Strenuous. None of the hikes in this book can be described as easy. The easiest are Segments Three and Seven which we have classified as Moderately Strenuous. Most are classified as Strenuous, and one (Segment One) is classified as Very Strenuous if hiked counterclockwise. We have not given a time for any of the hikes, recognizing that people vary in their hiking pace and in the time they like to spend enjoying the scenery, identifying the flowers, taking photographs, and just lingering. All should be considered full day hikes.

CAR SECURITY

Unfortunately, theft from cars has become a real problem at many trailheads. It is not a good idea to leave *anything* valuable in the car.

ACCESS and PERMITS

A new program goes into effect Jan. 1, 1998,
requiring a *Trail Park Pass* windshield sticker for
all vehicles parked at designated trailheads in the
Mt Hood National Forest . These passes will cost
$3.00 for a day, or $25.00 for an annual pass. A
second pass can be purchased for $5.00 for an
additional vehicle registered to an individual, if
purchased at the same time as the annual pass.
Passes can be purchased at National Forest offices
and visitor centers (and probably some local
businesses).

The Forest Service is also developing a plan to
limit the number of people who use the
Timberline Trail at any one time. The goal is to
meet a wilderness standard, defined in terms of
the number of hiking groups an individual will see
in an 8-hour day. Until this plan goes into effect,
hikers are required to register at the Wilderness
Permit Boxes and to carry a copy of their permit
with them.

Present regulations limit groups hiking in the Mt
Hood National Forest to 12. This includes
recreational animals, such as horses (not dogs).

HIKING SAFETY

None of these trails should be considered easy, or appropriate for very young children or adults who are not reasonably fit. They all involve hiking at or around the timber line which is certainly more taxing than hiking at sea level. Hiking on Mt Hood should not be taken lightly; the weather can change unexpectedly and there are no places to go for help on the trail, apart from Timberline Lodge and, perhaps, Cloud Cap.

It is a good idea to take extra clothing, food and water, however briefly you expect to be out on the trail. Even better is getting in the habit of keeping a small hiking kit packed with hiking essentials, and taking it with you whenever you go out on the trails. The Mazamas recommends the following
10 Essentials:
Whistle
Map
Compass
Flashlight
Extra food and clothing (including rain gear)
First Aid Kit
Matches in waterproof container
Firestarter or candle
Sunglasses & sun/windburn screen

For safety in the fall, after the hunting season has started, a day-glo orange hat may make the difference between you and the deer being bagged!

IT IS NOT A GOOD IDEA TO HIKE ALONE. If you do, you might want to consider taking a cellular phone—and be sure to tell someone where you are going! The cell phone should only be used to call for help if there is a true emergency. To use it otherwise is to waste the precious resources of the Forest Service and other groups involved in mountain rescues.

MAPS

It is a good idea to get in the habit of carrying and using a map when in the mountains. We recommend the Mt Hood Wilderness Map that is readily available at many bookstores, outdoor stores and the US Forest Service Information Centers. We also recommend the Green Trails Maps for the hikes in this book because they give accurate information about the access roads. Some of the segments need two of the Green Trails Maps. The USGS maps are a little less useful for the Timberline Trail because they are bigger and almost all of the segments need more than one map.

RIVER CROSSINGS

All but two of the segments of the Timberline Trail involve at least one river crossing. Only two of the rivers have bridges; the others have to be forded. The crossings can be intimidating because the water is extremely cold and the rivers are swift running and often turbulent. They aren't very wide, however. Don't be intimidated, but on the other hand, treat them with respect. With care, none of them should pose a major problem for people who are reasonably nimble. Extra care is needed with young children. The safest strategy is to take a rope, secure it to the person who is crossing, and hold on to the other end. If there is a spill, there is something to hold on to. A walking stick, ski pole or strong branch can provide a lot of stability.

There are different schools of thought about footwear: boots on or off. We find the boots-on-socks-off technique works the best. This provides the maximum stability for footing and the boots dry easily, perhaps helped with a wipe from a bandana. Some who prefer the barefoot approach can handle the rocks and hidden hazards. A popular solution, especially with backpackers who have heavy packs, and those with leather boots, is to take a light pair of canvas shoes or waterproof sandals.

WATER

Unfortunately, it is not safe to drink the water from the streams, lakes and ponds on Mt Hood because many of the streams have become contaminated. To be on the safe side, carry the water you need for a day hike (and don't underestimate!) or take purifying tablets to treat the water. If camping, use purifying tablets, a purification pump, or bring water to a rolling boil for five minutes.

WEATHER

Although the weather on Mt Hood in the summer is usually delightful, it is important to remember that weather in the mountains can change very suddenly. At the altitude of the Timberline Trail, snow may fall any month of the year. So, be prepared! Always take extra—and appropriate— clothes in case of rain and wind. And remember to take sun protection and dark glasses.

ANIMALS & BIRDS

About 40 species of mammals are residents of Mt Hood, ranging from squirrels, shrews, marmots, and weasels, to coyotes, black bear, mountain lions, deer and elk. Most are glimpsed very rarely because they are very shy. Black flies or no-see-ums can pose an incredible irritation on some portions of the trail, especially early in the summer when the snow is still melting, or just melted. The worst spots are near the streams. Almost 150 species of birds have been observed around Mt Hood.

ABOUT MT HOOD

Mt Hood, rising 11,235 ft. above sea level and 9500 ft. above the Hood River Valley, is the tallest peak in Oregon. It is one of a string of volcanoes, stretching from Mt Lassen in northern California to Mt Garibaldi in British Columbia, that have arisen from intense friction between the Pacific and American tectonic plates. That at least is the geological explanation for its magnificent presence. There are other, perhaps more romantic and colorful explanations.

According to an Indian legend, there was once a great natural bridge spanning the Columbia River, near the town now called Cascade Locks. The land was ruled by the supernaturally powerful sons of the Great Spirit: Pahto to the north of the bridge and Wy'East to the south. The braves fell in love with the same maiden but she could not decide which she preferred. So the braves fought a savage battle for her affection, hurling fire and hot stones at each other across the river and devastating the countryside. The "Bridge of the Gods" collapsed, so angering the Great Spirit that he turned his sons into guardians of the Columbia. Wy'East became Mt Hood and Pahto became Mt Adams. The maiden became Mt St. Helens.

According to another legend, Paul Bunyon pitched camp one night six strides east of the falls on the Willamette and uprooted a handful of trees to build a roaring fire. In the morning he covered the embers with a huge pile of rocks and soil and sprinkled on some snow, thereby inadvertently forming Mt Hood.

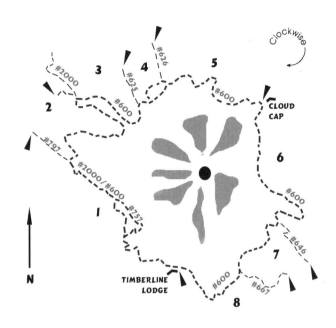

LIST OF SEGMENTS

I TIMBERLINE LODGE -- RAMONA FALLS TRAILHEAD

2 RAMONA FALLS TRAILHEAD -- TOP SPUR TRAILHEAD

3 TOP SPUR TRAILHEAD -- MAZAMA TRAILHEAD

4 MAZAMA TRAILHEAD -- VISTA RIDGE TRAILHEAD

5 VISTA RIDGE TRAILHEAD -- CLOUD CAP

6 CLOUD CAP -- SAHALIE FALLS TRAILHEAD

7 SAHALIE FALLS TRAILHEAD -- UMBRELLA FALLS TRAILHEAD

8 UMBRELLA FALLS TRAILHEAD -- TIMBERLINE LODGE

LIST OF TRAILS SHOWN ON THE MAPS

600   TIMBERLINE TRAIL

600A   TILLY JANE CAMPGROUND TRAIL

600B   COOPER SPUR TRAIL

600H   EDEN PARK TRAIL

600M   MCNEIL POINT TRAIL

625   MAZAMA TRAIL (CATHEDRAL RIDGE TRAIL)

626   VISTA RIDGE TRAIL

627   MCGEE CREEK TRAIL

630   PINNACLE RIDGE TRAIL

631   ELK COVE TRAIL

645   ELK MEADOWS TRAIL

646   NEWTON CREEK TRAIL

652   GNARL RIDGE TRAIL

667   UMBRELLA FALLS TRAIL

757   PARADISE PARK LOOP

771   YOKUM RIDGE TRAIL

778   PARADISE PARK TRAIL

779   HIDDEN LAKE TRAIL

784   BALD MOUNTAIN TRAIL

784A   TOP SPUR TRAIL

797   RAMONA FALLS TRAIL

798   MOUNTAINEER TRAIL

2000   PACIFIC CREST TRAIL

HOW TO GET TO MT HOOD

The major access roads to Mt Hood are Hwy 26 to the south and I-84 to the north (see map on page 16). For most of the segments we have given instructions from both the north and south. Segments 1,2,3,7 and 8 are probably most easily accessed from Hwy 26. The others can be accessed from either direction.

Since the access roads around the mountain are not shown on Oregon highway maps, we recommend that you have a more detailed map to help you negotiate the back roads. The best available at present is the Mt Hood Wilderness Map available at many bookstores, outdoor stores, and at the U.S. Forest Service Information Centers. The Mt Hood Information Center in Wemme on Hwy 26 is open on weekends; the Information Center in Mt Hood Village on Hwy 35 is closed on weekends.

If taking Hwy 26 east from Portland:
Take I-84 east from Portland to the Wood Village exit, about 15 miles from the city center. Turn right through Wood Village, continue for about 3 miles into Gresham, and turn left onto Burnside. In about a mile, Burnside becomes Hwy 26.

If taking I-84 in either direction:
either... Take the West Hood River exit 62, continue for 1.1 miles, turn right on 13th Street, and follow signs for Odell. After 8 miles, cross a bridge, turn right, and continue straight at a Y-junction for another 4 miles to a fork. Take the right fork to Dee, and follow signs to Lost Lake. Continue, now on Road 13, through Dee, to the junctions of Roads 13 and 18, another 8 miles. Take the left fork, now on Hwy 18.

Or... Take the Hwy 35 Exit in Hood River and drive south on Hwy 35.

LEGEND FOR THE MAPS

▲ **CAMPGROUND**

GLACIER OR LAKE

LODGE OR VISITOR CENTER

RIDGE OR CANYON

RIVERS & LARGER STREAMS

ROADS

SHELTER

#600 **TRAIL NUMBERS**

TRAILS (MAIN HIKE SEGMENT IS LARGER)

↑ **TRUE NORTH**

Mt Hood was named on October 29, 1792 by Lt. William Broughton, the leader of a British expedition, who saw "A very distant high snowy mountain..." as the expedition was sailing up the Columbia. It was named in honor of Rear Admiral Samuel Hood, a very distinguished officer in the British Navy. Lewis and Clark reported seeing Mt Hood for the first time on October 18, 1805.

Area Map of Roads

Campgrounds	Water	Fee	Road	Spots
Alpine			173	16
Badger Lake			4860-140	15
Barlow Creek			3530	5
Bonney Crossing			43-3530	8
Bonney Meadows			2710	5
Boulder Lake			4880	4
Camp Creek	·	·	26	24
Camp Windy			3550	2
Clear Lake	·	·	2630	28
Cloud Cap Saddle	·		3512	3
Devil's Half Acre			3530	5
Eightmile Crossing			4430	18
Fifteenmile			2730	3
Forest Creek			4885	8
Frog Lake	·	·	2610	33
Gibson Prairie Horse Camp			17	4
Green Canyon	·	·	2618	15
Grindstone			3530	5
Knebal Springs Horse Camp			1720	8
Little Badger			2710	3
Lost Creek	·	·	1825	9
Lost Lake	·	·	1340	91
McNeil		·	1825	34
Pebble Ford			44	3
Rainy Lake			2820	4
Riley Horse Camp	·	·	1825	14
Robinhood	·	·	35	24
Sherwood	·	·	36	14
Still Creek	·	·	26	27
Tilly Jane			3512	14
Tollgate	·	·	26	15
Trillium Lake	·	·	2656	54
Wahtum Lake			1310	5
White River Station			3530	5
Timothy Lake	·	·	2618	15

Reservations: 5 days in advance
                  1-800-280-2267
                  1-301-722-9101 (from outside the US)
                  1-301-722-9802 (fax)

SEGMENT ONE
TIMBERLINE LODGE -- RAMONA FALLS TRAILHEAD

> *FEATURES: Dramatic views of the canyons carved by the branches of the Sandy River; huckleberries galore in late August; magnificent alpine meadows on the Paradise Park Loop.*

DIFFICULTY: Strenuous
because of the distance, not elevation gain, if hiked *clockwise*; **Very Strenuous** for both reasons if hiked *counterclockwise*.

DISTANCE: 12.6 miles one way
Elevation Gain : 1000 ft. if hiked clockwise from Timberline Lodge; **3200 ft.** if hiked counterclockwise from Ramona Falls Trailhead.

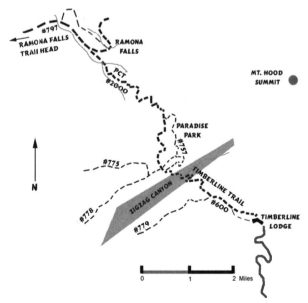

18

MAPS:
Mt Hood Wilderness Map;
Green Trails: Mt Hood #462,
Government Camp # 461;
USGS: Government Camp, Mt Hood South,
Bull Run Lake

DESCRIPTION: This is the longest segment, but a relatively easy one if hiked clockwise (Timberline Lodge to Ramona Falls Trailhead) because most of the distance is downhill. If hiked counterclockwise, however, the hike is both long and involves an appreciable elevation gain. Since Timberline Lodge is at one end of the hike, most of the hike (all but 2.9 miles) is on the Timberline Trail. The hike does

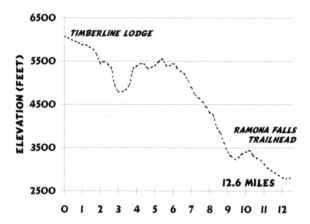

involve a river crossing (Sandy River), but this is usually manageable. This section offers spectacular views of Mt Hood, the glaciers on the south side, and the canyons carved by the origins of the Sandy River. The views over the Salmon Huckleberry Wilderness and south to Mt Jefferson are also dramatic. Wildflowers are plentiful, especially around the streams. A worthwhile add-on up to Paradise Park (an additional 720 ft.) offers an extravagant display of flowers in a magnificent setting.

CLOCKWISE OR COUNTERCLOCKWISE?

This is not a hard decision! The clockwise direction (Timberline Lodge to Ramona Falls Trailhead) is a relatively easy hike with considerably more elevation loss than gain; the counterclockwise direction is a hard workout with 3200 ft. elevation gain. For the counterclockwise direction, the uphill

Sandy River Canyon

sections are at the beginning and at the end. So, make your choice based on how much you want to work. One important consideration is the difficulty of the Sandy River crossing: if you are hiking clockwise, the crossing comes towards the end of an already long hike. It's a long hike back if you find the crossing is too scary (though this is unlikely). This is usually one of the easier river crossings on the Timberline Trail. (See the Introduction for a

Crossing the
Sandy River

discussion of different
techniques of river
crossing which may help
to ease anxiety.) The
views are great in both
directions.

Monkeyflower

RIVER CROSSING:

There is one river
crossing of the Sandy
River. As with all of the
river crossings on the Timberline Trail, the amount
of water, and therefore the difficulty, can vary
appreciably depending on the snow melt, time of
day, and time of year (usually more challenging
earlier in the summer, e.g. June/July, when the river
is fuller). The Sandy River at this crossing is usually
no more than 25-30 ft. wide and is not usually very
turbulent or deep, so is not particularly scary or
difficult. But, as always with river crossings, care is
needed.

CAR SHUTTLE OR CAR SWAP: This hike works
well with a car shuttle or car swap. The shuttle is
neither long nor difficult but it will add an extra
hour at the beginning and end of the day. If you
plan to do a car shuttle and are driving from
Portland, dropping a car off at the Ramona Falls
Trailhead and taking the second car up to
Timberline Lodge is probably most efficient. It is
also the easier option. If you are doing a car swap,
remember to take a spare key in case you manage
to miss each other on the trail.

TRAILHEADS: If hiking clockwise, park at
Timberline Lodge; if hiking counterclockwise, park
at the Ramona Falls Trailhead parking area. Both
trailheads are reached from Hwy 26: the Timberline
Lodge parking lot is 5.2 miles from Hwy 26; the
Ramona Falls parking lot is 7.2 miles from Hwy 26.

To reach Timberline Lodge:

If driving from Portland, drive east on Hwy 26 through Gresham, Sandy, Wemme, Zigzag, Rhododendron and past Government Camp. The road to Timberline Lodge takes off to the left (north) just after the Summit Rest Area at the far (east) end of the Government Camp loop.

If driving from Hood River, drive south on Hwy 35, then west on Hwy 26 towards Government Camp. The access road to Timberline Lodge is on the right (north), just before the Summit Rest Area at the east end of the Government Camp loop. The parking areas for the Lodge are 5.2 miles up the access road.

To reach the Ramona Falls Trailhead:

If driving from Portland, drive east on Hwy 26 through Gresham, Sandy and Wemme. In Zigzag, turn left (north) onto the Lolo Pass Road.

If driving from Hood River, drive south on Hwy 35 and west on Hwy 26, through Government Camp to Zigzag. Turn right (north) onto the Lolo Pass Road 18.

Continue on the Lolo Pass Road for 4.3 miles, turn right on Road 1825, signed to McNeil and Riley Campgrounds and Lost Creek Trail, and stay on Road 1825 for 2.4 miles to a fork. Take the left fork signed to the Ramona Falls Trail # 797; the right fork is signed to Lost Creek. The road ends in a large parking area. There used to be access to the Ramona Falls Trail up a very bad road, but this was closed after the storms in 1996 made it even more impassable. Access is now by a trail from the parking area.

CLOCKWISE: *TIMBERLINE LODGE TO RAMONA FALLS TRAILHEAD*

The Timberline Trail (#600) runs together with the Pacific Crest Trail (#2000) from Timberline Lodge and is signed as the Pacific Crest Trail (PCT) on this segment.

There are two ways to pick up the Timberline Trail/ PCT when heading west: from the Lodge, take the upper paved road, just above the Magic Mile Lift, and where the road forks just past the lift, either continue on up the right paved fork, following the signs for the Pacific Crest Trail, or take the left fork, just after the lift, and immediately look for a sign for the Mountaineer Trail. The Mountaineer Trail and the Timberline Trail/PCT join after about 0.7 mile.

*Be sure to sign in at the **Wilderness Permit Box 1 mile from Timberline Lodge.***

Picking huckleberries is an added bonus along this trail!

Continue on the PCT heading west, passing the trail to Hidden Lake (#779) 1.4 miles from the Lodge, and dipping in and out of two shallow canyons (Sand and Little Zigzag) and one deep canyon (Zigzag). The trail drops 750 ft. into Zigzag Canyon, and 3.3 miles from Timberline Lodge, crosses the headwaters of the Zigzag River (here only a stream), and climbs back out of the canyon.

About ¼ mile from the bottom of the canyon, before you reach the top, the trail divides: the right fork climbs for another 1½ miles and 720 ft. to Paradise Park; the left is the continuation of the combined Timberline Trail/PCT. Take the right fork through Paradise Park for a higher route, mostly above the timber line, with spectacular flowers and alpine meadows. This route does not add any distance, but involves an additional 720 ft. climb (quite steep), so if you need to conserve your strength for the distance ahead, continue straight. If you have to forego the extra climb to Paradise Park, promise yourself that you will return because these meadows are among the most magnificent of the many alpine meadows on Mt Hood.

The trail continues to climb, but at an easy grade. Ignore the Paradise Park Trail (#778) that starts in Paradise Park and crosses the PCT. The Paradise Park Loop Trail and Timberline Trail/PCT join again after about 2½ miles. Continue straight on the PCT and soon begin the long descent into the canyon carved by the Sandy River.

This section of the trail is lined by huckleberry bushes, usually laden with succulent berries in August. The views of Mt Hood from this part of the trail are very different from most of the other views: the lower flanks are covered with bushes and have a velvety green hue, compared to the grey rock of most of the rest of the lower flanks of the mountain. Before the trail enters the forest, there are dramatic views of the Sandy River Canyon, carved by two branches of the river, and a little further, of the canyon carved by Rushing Water Creek, another branch of the Sandy River. The trail drops in gradual

Huckleberries

bends to the Sandy River, and then follows downstream for a short distance to a crossing place marked by cairns. This is the lowest point of the Timberline Trail (3200 ft.). Cross with care, find the resumption of the trail on the far bank, and climb gradually to the top of the west canyon wall. The trail joins the Ramona Falls Trail (#797) at a T-junction. The most direct way to the trailhead is to take the left fork which is the left arm of the Ramona Falls Loop. A very beautiful (and slightly longer) alternative is to take the right fork and the right arm of the Ramona Falls Loop which passes Ramona Falls (see map).

Follow either arm of the Ramona Falls Loop to a 4-way intersection and take the fork that goes downstream. The trail soon meets the Sandy River where there is usually a sturdy bridge. At the far side, the trail continues more or less beside, or parallel to, the river and between the old road and the river. The parking lot is 1.3 miles through lovely open forest with beautiful moss-covered rocks.

COUNTERCLOCKWISE: *RAMONA FALLS TRAILHEAD TO TIMBERLINE LODGE*

The first 2.9 miles of the trail is the Ramona Falls Trail # 797. The trailhead is at the north (mountain) side of the parking lot, just after the entrance, and is signed to the Sandy River Trail (¼ mile) and the Ramona Falls Trail (1¼ miles) and designated for the use of hikers, horses and bikes.

This first part of the trail runs between the old road and the Sandy River, through open forest with moss-covered rocks that almost beg to be stroked. In some places, it splits and you can walk up the old road or continue on the trail, close to the river. Ignore the fork on the left that goes to the river, ¼ mile from the parking area. The place where you cross the river is well marked (no bikes from here; hikers and horses only). Cross the bridge(s) and find the trail at the far side, signed to Ramona Falls #797, and walk a short distance further to a confluence of four trails.

Continue straight and sign in at the Wilderness Permit Box.

The trail climbs at a very gentle grade through open forest with many rhododendrons and with the river always within earshot on the right. 1.6 miles from the river crossing, the trail meets the combined Pacific Crest Trail (PCT) #2000 and Timberline Trail (#600), which are running together at this point.

Take the right fork, now on the Timberline Trail / PCT (the left fork is still #797 and continues to Ramona Falls), to the Sandy River crossing. This is the lowest point of the Timberline Trail (3200 ft.). The river is usually only 25-30 ft. wide at the crossing point and is not usually scarily turbulent or deep. Look for the resumption of the trail on the far bank (usually marked by a cairn), and follow it upstream for a short distance before it enters the forest and starts to climb. The next section of the trail climbs through the forest for about 2½ miles, mostly at a comfortable grade, and passes viewpoints with dramatic views of the Rushing Water Creek, a branch of the Sandy River.

The trail emerges from the forest onto an open area with another dramatic view of branches of the

Sandy River which have carved deep canyons. The views of the mountain here are different from most of the other parts of the mountain at this elevation because the lower flanks here are a soft, velvety green from a covering of bushes; quite a stark comparison to the usual grey rock and sand. There are plentiful bushes in this open area too: mostly mountain ash and huckleberries, usually laden with succulent berries in August. The trail continues upwards in the open area and forks. The left fork is part of the Paradise Park Loop (#757); the Timberline Trail/PCT continues straight and starts down at a gentle grade.

The next section of the trail more or less follows the contours of the mountain with little elevation gain or loss. The Paradise Park Trail (#778) crosses the Timberline Trail about 2½ miles from the intersection with the north end of the Paradise Loop Trail. From this point, the trail starts to drop more steeply to Zigzag Canyon. Ignore the southern intersection of the Paradise Park Loop (#757) on the left, 0.1 mile after the Paradise Park Trail (#778) crosses the main trail. The Zigzag River crossing is 3.3 miles from Timberline Lodge. The trail climbs back out of Zigzag Canyon and heads over to Timberline Lodge across mostly open meadows that are ski runs in the winter.

Phlox

There are only two more trail intersections: Hidden Lake Trail (#779), 1.9 miles from the Zigzag River crossing, and Mountaineer Trail (#798) after another 0.6 miles. You can either continue on Timberline Trail or take the Mountaineer Trail fork to the right. Both will lead to Timberline Lodge in about 0.7 mile.

Trillium

Elijah (Lige) Coalman *was a legendary climbing guide on Mt Hood. There are probably more stories about his adventures than about anyone else's. His first ascent was in 1897 at the age of 15; his last (and 586th) was in 1928. He established a lookout on the summit of Mt Hood and manned it for the Forest Service for four seasons, often giving tea and hot soup to exhausted climbers. The stories about the injured climbers he helped are almost unbelievable, as are his feats of climbing up to the summit and glissading down. In 1912, he climbed from the old cabin near Timberline Lodge to the summit in 98 minutes; in 1917, he slid and ran down from the summit to the treeline in 13 minutes, to help a friend who had been seriously hurt.*

Timberline Lodge

Timberline Lodge provides a convenient starting point for many hikes. Parking is easy. The main Lodge and Wy'east Day Lodge offer a range of options for refreshments, plus a gift shop and ski rental area. Timberline Lodge itself is a remarkable and impressive building and well worth a visit.

Built in the mid-1930s as a project of the Works Progress Administration, it has been lovingly maintained and restored by the US Forest Service, Friends of Timberline, and the RLK Corporation. It is a wonderful place to stay or just to linger and enjoy the ambience. The handcrafted furnishings are perfectly suited to the Lodge and its setting, and the views in every direction are stunning. Function, art and whimsy combine to make the inside of the Lodge striking. The staircase newel posts are carved in the form of a variety of animals that invite you to touch and fondle them.

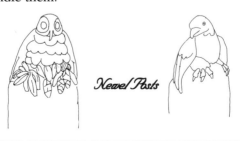

Newel Posts

SEGMENT TWO

RAMONA FALLS TRAILHEAD -- TOP SPUR TRAILHEAD

> **FEATURES:** *This section includes Ramona Falls, one of the favorite falls in Oregon. The views of Mt Hood from the Muddy Fork area and Bald Mountain are very impressive because the trail is relatively low in this section, so the mountain looks awesomely high and steep and there are many waterfalls cascading down the cliffs.*

DIFFICULTY: Moderately Strenuous
because of the river crossings, not the hiking.

DISTANCE: 9.3 miles one way
Elevation Gain : 1950 ft. if hiked clockwise from
Ramona Falls Trailhead; **800 ft.** if hiked
counterclockwise from Top Spur Trailhead.

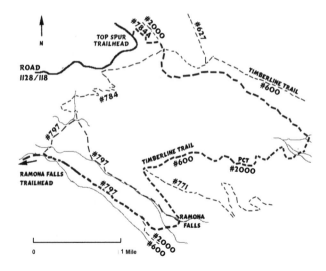

MAPS:
Mt. Hood Wilderness Map;
Green Trails: Mt. Hood #462, Gov't Camp #461

DESCRIPTION: A relatively easy section of the Timberline Trail that entails little elevation gain or loss but requires two crossings of branches of the Muddy Fork of the Sandy River. This section is all below the timber line, and mostly through shady forest with frequent small streams coming down to, or crossing, the trail so it is ideal for a hot day. It is one of the earliest sections to be snow-free, so it can usually be hiked in early July. Wild flowers are abundant, both in the forest and in the open sections. The views of Mt Hood, especially in the area of the river crossings, are spectacular.

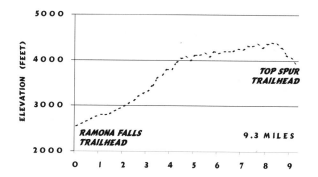

CLOCKWISE OR COUNTERCLOCKWISE?

Both directions are equally interesting. The clockwise direction has more elevation gain (1950 ft. vs. 800 ft.), but neither is strenuous as far as the hiking goes. One potentially important consideration is the river crossings: these come towards the end of the hike when hiking clockwise, but relatively early in the hike when hiking counterclockwise. If you are concerned about these, consider hiking counterclockwise.

*View of
Sandy Glacier,
McNeil Point,
and Muddy Fork*

RIVER CROSSINGS:

The crossings of the Muddy Fork branches can be sporting in July because of the snow melt, but most adults and older children who are strong and fit enough to do this hike should not find them too intimidating. Neither is usually more than 10-15 ft. wide but the water is exceedingly cold and turbulent. The crossings become easier later in the

summer as the snow melt slows down. To be on the safe side, and especially if you are hiking with children, consider taking a rope and securing it to the person who is crossing so that a stumble can be quickly corrected. A strong stick or ski pole can also provide some security. See the Introduction for a discussion of the different techniques of river crossing.

CAR SHUTTLE OR CAR SWAP: This hike works well as a car shuttle or car swap. The shuttle is neither long nor difficult but will add an extra 3/4 hour at the beginning and end of the day. If you are doing a car swap, remember to take a spare key for the other car in case you manage to miss each other on the trail.

TRAILHEADS:
If hiking clockwise, park at the Ramona Falls Trailhead; if hiking counterclockwise, park at the Top Spur Trailhead. Both trailheads are accessed from the Lolo Pass Road #18. which joins Hwy 26 at Zigzag.

If taking Hwy 26 east from Portland, pass through Gresham, Sandy and Wemme, to Zigzag. Turn left (north) onto the Lolo Pass Road 18.

chocolate lily

If taking I-84, take the Hwy 35 exit in Hood River, drive south, then west on Hwy 26 through Government Camp to Zigzag and turn right (north) onto the Lolo Pass Road 18.

Then...
Continue on the Lolo Pass Road for 4.3 miles to a fork, take the right fork, Road 1825, signed to McNeil and Riley Campgrounds and Lost Creek Trail and continue for almost 0.7 miles to where the road bends to the right and goes over a bridge.

To Reach the Ramona Falls Trailhead:
Cross the bridge and pass McNeil and Riley horse camps. Where the road forks at 1.7 miles after the

bridge, take the left fork signed to the Ramona Falls
Trail #797; the right fork is signed to Lost Creek.
The roads ends in a large parking area. There used
to be a very bad road up to the trailhead but it was
closed after the 1996 storms made it even more
impassable.

To Reach the Top Spur Trailhead:

Just before the bridge, the road divides. Keep
straight, now on a narrow side road 1828. Follow
Road 1828, which soon turns to gravel, for 5.7 miles
to a fork, ignoring several side roads. Take the right
fork and continue for another 1.6 miles. The
trailhead is on the right of the road, and there is
usually ample parking beside the road.

CLOCKWISE: *RAMONA FALLS TRAILHEAD TO TOP SPUR TRAILHEAD*

The first 2.9 miles of the trail that leads up to the
Timberline Trail is the Ramona Falls Trail #797. The
trailhead is at the north (mountain) side of the
parking lot, just after the entrance, and is signed to
the Sandy River Trail (¼ mile), and the Ramona Falls
Trail (1¼ miles) and is designated for the use of
hikers, horses and bikes.

This first part of the trail runs between the old road
and the Sandy River, through open forest with richly
moss-covered rocks that almost beg to be stroked.
In some places, the trail splits and you can walk up
the old road or continue close to the river. Ignore
the spur on the left, ¼ mile from the parking lot.

Twinflowers

Solomon's Seal

The place where you cross the river is well marked
(no bikes from here; hikers and horses only). Cross
on the bridge(s), find the trail at the far side, signed
to Ramona Falls #797, and walk a short distance
parallel to the river to a confluence of four trails.
Continue straight across the 4-way intersection.

***Remember to sign in at the Wilderness
Registration Box***.

The trail climbs at a very gentle grade through open
forest with many rhododendrons and with the river
on the right, always within earshot. This portion of
the trail is very dry and mostly devoid of flowers. In
July, however, twin flowers cover portions of the
banks. 1.3 miles from the river crossing, the trail
meets the combined Pacific Crest Trail (PCT) #2000
and Timberline Trail #600, which are running
together at this point.

Keep left, now on the combined Timberline Trail/
PCT, and continue for another ½ mile to the
dramatic Ramona Falls. Cross the bridge and start
down the other arm of the Ramona Falls Loop.
Almost immediately the trail forks: take the right
fork.

There are far more flowers on this section of the
trail and the forest is rich with rhododendrons.
Look for anemones, inside-out flowers, Mt Hood

lilies, bunchberry, and pipsissewa in the drier sections and yellow monkey flowers, bog orchids, and Solomon's Seal and moss in the wetter sections. After 0.6 miles, the Yokum Ridge Trail (#771) takes off to the right. Continue straight on the Timberline Trail/PCT, still climbing very gently. The trail may be a bit precarious in places if the winter has

Beargrass

been harsh and streams have washed out parts of the trail, but it is mostly very easy hiking.

The only challenge comes with the two crossings of the Muddy Fork of the Sandy River. The first is the more difficult because the river is narrower and more turbulent. Take your time to find a good fording place. If you belong to the boots-on-socks-off school of river crossing (see the Introduction for river crossing techniques), keep your socks off until you have crossed the second branch. This is usually quite a bit easier than the first crossing, but still needs care.

Be sure to take the time to look up at the mountain and the waterfalls cascading off the sheer cliffs. After the river crossings, the trail continues to climb gently, still through the forest, before emerging onto the open hillside of Bald Mountain, ablaze with flowers by mid July. A short distance after the trail re-enters the forest, there is another trail junction where the Timberline and Pacific Crest Trails part; the PCT continuing straight, the Timberline Trail turning sharply to the right. Continue straight on the PCT.

You are now leaving the Timberline Trail but are still on the PCT for about 50 yards to the junction of the PCT and Top Spur Trail (#784A). Take the left fork onto Top Spur Trail. The trailhead is another ½ mile down through beautiful forest with rhododendrons, beargrass, clintonia, cat's ears, lupines, Indian paintbrush, huckleberry bushes and inside-out flowers. The beargrass in this section of the forest is particularly spectacular in a good beargrass year.

COUNTERCLOCKWISE: *TOP SPUR TRAILHEAD TO RAMONA FALLS TRAILHEAD*

The trail climbs gently from the road through beautiful forest with rhododendrons, beargrass, clintonia, anemones, cat's ears, lupines, Indian paintbrush, huckleberry bushes and inside out flowers. Listen for the hermit thrush.

Cascade Lily

After ½ mile, turn right at a T-junction onto the Pacific Crest Trail (PCT) #2000, signed to Ramona Falls, and walk a short distance to a 4-trail junction. Continue straight, now on the combined Timberline Trail/PCT.

Remember to sign in at the Wilderness Permit Box.

Continue for a short distance on a trail that is initially flat or gently uphill, then emerges onto an open hillside ablaze with flowers. The next section is a garden of wildflowers: delphiniums, potentilla, wild roses, paintbrush, yellow violets, bleeding heart, Cascade lilies and vivid yellow monkey flowers.

The trail continues either flat or gently downhill and enters a quiet forest clinging to a steep hillside. The soft pine needles cushion your step. The trail emerges from the forest and crosses the first of several branches of the Muddy Fork of the Sandy River. The first is just a small stream. The next is a boisterous, fast-flowing torrent in early summer and needs care to ford. (See the Introduction for river crossing techniques). Look up and see the dramatic waterfalls cascading off the cliffs ahead of you. The next crossing is the more challenging because the river is deeper and more turbulent. That is the last challenge!

The rest of the trail is very straightforward and continues along the same contour, mostly flat. There are lovely vistas of forested slopes and Mt Hood. This section of the trail has more snow runoff than the earlier section so there are many small streams crossing the trail, pretty waterfalls and abundant wildflowers.

The trail enters another stretch of quiet forest, rich with rhododendrons, and drops gently to intersect with the Ramona Falls Loop Trail # 797. At the intersection you can take either arm of the loop

Penstemon

> **LOOP OPTION:** *This hike can easily be made into a loop by taking the Bald Mountain Trail #784 (see map).*

(see map); both are equally beautiful. To see the dramatic falls, take the left fork. Then either continue on past the falls for another ½ mile and take the right (south) fork, now leaving the Timberline Trail, or return to the fork before the falls and follow the right arm of the Ramona Falls Loop.

Either arm of the Ramona Falls Loop will bring you to a 4-way intersection. Take the fork that heads downstream. The trail soon meets the Sandy River where there is usually a sturdy bridge. At the far side, the trail continues more or less parallel to the river, between the old road and the river. The parking lot is 1.3 miles through lovely open forest with beautiful moss-covered rocks.

Coral Root

SEGMENT THREE

TOP SPUR TRAILHEAD -- MAZAMA TRAILHEAD

FEATURES: *The section of this hike that is on the Timberline Trail has some of the most spectacular displays of flowers and alpine meadows of the whole Timberline Trail. The many streams are lined by multicolored masses of monkeyflowers, paintbrush, marsh marigolds and, later in the summer, by gentians.*

DIFFICULTY: Moderately Strenuous
modest elevation gain, no river crossing.

DISTANCE: 6.6 miles one way
Elevation Gain : 1680 ft. if hiked clockwise from
Top Spur Trailhead; **2080 ft.** if hiked
counterclockwise from Mazama Trailhead.

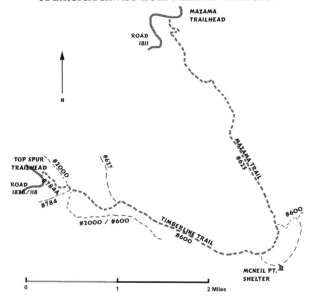

DESCRIPTION: This is one of the easiest segments, and also one of the most scenic. Only 3 miles of this segment are on the Timberline Trail (#600); the rest is on the access trails, Top Spur Trail (#784A) for ½ mile and Mazama Trail (#625) for 3.1 miles. All of the sections of this hike, however, are beautiful and interesting. The segment of the hike that is on the Timberline Trail is one of the most popular and most spectacular, so don't expect to whizz along without any stops; the scenery is breathtaking and the meadows are ablaze with wildflowers.

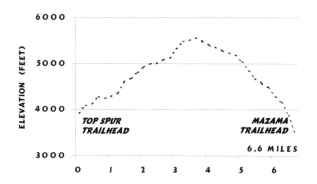

If you would like to make this hike a little longer and more challenging, climb the extra 700 ft. to the McNeil Point Shelter and continue on the high trail that will lead you back to the main trail. This adds a steep climb and great views but misses out on some of the exquisite meadows and flowers along the main, lower trail. If you do chose the higher route, note that you have to backtrack a little (counterclockwise) to find the Mazama Trail, once you are back on the Timberline Trail.

CLOCKWISE OR COUNTERCLOCKWISE?

This hike works well
from either direction.
The access trail is shorter
when going clockwise
(Top Spur to Mazama
Trail), so the spectacular
views and alpine
meadows come sooner.
This may be a
consideration if the
weather is likely to
change.

Cat's Ear Lilies

RIVER CROSSING: None

CAR SHUTTLE OR CAR SWAP:
This hike works well with a car shuttle or car swap.
The shuttle adds about an extra hour at the
beginning and end of the day, but is not long or
difficult. If you are doing a car swap, remember to
take a spare car key for the other car in case you
manage to miss each other on the way.

TRAILHEADS: If hiking clockwise, park at the Top
Spur Trailhead; if hiking counterclockwise, park at
the Mazama Trailhead. Both trailheads are accessed
from the Lolo Pass Road 18 which joins Hwy 26 at
Zigzag. The Top Spur Trailhead is 12.3 miles from
Hwy 26, the Mazama Trailhead is 18.4 miles.

If taking Hwy 26 east from Portland, pass
through Gresham, Sandy and Wemme, to Zigzag.
Turn left (north) onto the Lolo Pass Road 18.

If taking I-84, take the Hwy 35 exit in Hood
River, drive south on Hwy 35, then west on Hwy 26
through Government Camp to Zigzag and turn right
(north) onto the Lolo Pass Road 18.

To reach the Top Spur Trailhead:

Continue on the Lolo Pass Road for 4.3 miles and take a right onto Road 1825, signed to McNeil and Riley Campgrounds and Lost Lake Trail. The road bends to the right and goes over a bridge 0.7 miles from the fork. Keep straight instead of crossing the bridge, now on a narrow road 1828, signed to Top Spur Trailhead 8 miles. Follow Road 1828, which soon turns to gravel, for 5.7 miles to a fork. Take the right fork and continue for another 1.6 miles. The Top Spur Trailhead is on the right of the road, and there is usually ample parking beside the road.

If continuing on to the Mazama Trailhead, go back 1.6 miles to the first fork (Road 1828), take the right fork, and drive 3 miles to the junction with the Lolo Pass Road. Turn right onto the Lolo Pass Road and almost immediately right again onto Road 1810. Drive 5.3 miles and turn right onto Road 1811. The Mazama Trailhead is another 2.4 miles.

Columbine

To reach the Mazama Trailhead:

Continue on the Lolo Pass Road for 10.7 miles to the top of Lolo Pass. Road 1828 joins Road 18 on the right, just at the top of Lolo Pass. This will be the road that you will be taking to go back to Top Spur Trailhead. Just after Road 1828 joins the Lolo Pass Road, turn right onto Road 1810, which is good quality, and after 5.3 miles, turn right again onto Road 1811. The Mazama Trailhead is another 2.4 miles and there is ample parking beside the road. If continuing on to the Top Spur Trailhead, return the same way to the top of Lolo Pass and Road 18. Turn left onto Road 18 and almost

immediately take another left onto Road 1828.
Continue on Road 1828 for 3.0 miles and take a left
at a Y-intersection, signed to Top Spur Trailhead,
ignoring a road to the right at 2.2 miles. The Top
Spur Trailhead is another 1.6 miles, on the right.

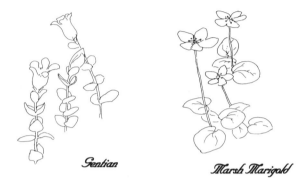

Gentian   *Marsh Marigold*

CLOCKWISE: *TOP SPUR TRAILHEAD TO*
MAZAMA TRAILHEAD

The Top Spur Trail (# 784A) climbs gently from the
road through beautiful forest with beargrass,
rhododendrons, clintonia, anemones, cat's ears,
lupines, Indian paintbrush, huckleberry bushes, and
inside-out flowers. Listen for the hermit thrush.
After ½ mile, turn right at a T-junction onto the
Pacific Crest Trail (#2000), signed to Ramona Falls,
and walk a short distance to a 4-way junction. Take
the first left fork onto the Timberline Trail (#600).

Continue, now on the Timberline Trail, through
beautiful forest, ignoring the McGee Creek Trail
(#627) that joins Timberline Trail on the left after ½
mile.

Clintonia

Remember to sign in at the Wilderness Permit Box, ¼ mile after the McGee Creek Trail joins the Timberline Trail.

About ¼ mile after the Wilderness Permit Box the trail emerges from the forest and follows along a ridge heading straight for Mt Hood. The views in every direction and the displays of flowers on the open slopes are so spellbinding that even the most hardened hiker has been heard to spontaneously break into oohs and aahs!

The trail continues to climb gently to the timber line, taking easy loops. Continue on the Timberline Trail, passing an unmarked trail to McNeil Point in an open meadow. If you are feeling energetic, the add-on loop up to McNeil Point is well worth the effort (see map, and below). Continue on the Timberline Trail climbing gently, crossing delectable streams lined with extravagant displays of wildflowers, and passing between two shallow lakes (which may dry up in August or September). The displays of gentians are particularly spectacular later in the summer. Keep an eye out for the turn onto the Mazama Trail on the left, soon after the lakes, as the trail emerges from the forest and Mt Hood appears again on the right. If you reach a Y-fork, you have gone too far. When you turn onto the Mazama Trail, you are leaving the Timberline Trail.

Avalanche Lilies

45

Turn left onto the Mazama Trail (# 625) and follow it down for 3.1 miles to the trailhead, mostly through fairly open forest. Just after the beginning of the Mazama Trail, there is a rock field on the right. Listen for the whistle of the little "rock rabbits", more correctly called pikas. The last mile is a steep series of zigzags, first through the forest, then through a steep rock field. By this time, though, you will be able to see the parking area and know that you are almost at the trailhead.

Snag at McNeil Point

COUNTERCLOCKWISE: *MAZAMA TRAILHEAD TO TOP SPUR TRAILHEAD*

Remember to sign in at the Wilderness Permit Box

The Mazama Trail (#625) starts at the parking lot and almost immediately starts to climb steeply, initially zigzagging up a field of rocks, then continuing to zigzag up to the crest of Cathedral Ridge through a hillside of rhododendron bushes. This part of the trail has been completely rebuilt by the Mazamas since it was badly damaged in the mid-1980's.

The trail continues through the forest up along

Cathedral Ridge, sometimes in shady forest, sometimes in more open forest. Stretches with steeper pitches are interspersed with more gentle stretches. The undergrowth up the ridge is brushy with rhododendrons, huckleberry, and some chinquapin. The beargrass in a good beargrass year is luxurious in the more open areas, and bunchberries and orchids are often plentiful in the more shady areas.

Continue steadily upwards for about two miles before the first dramatic views of the mountain appear directly ahead. Over the next mile, the trail goes through meadows white with avalanche lilies, and thick with beargrass, heather and mountain spirea, and the mountain comes steadily closer and more imposing. The last stretch before reaching the Timberline Trail is in the forest, along the side of the ridge with a steep dropoff to the right, then beside a rock field on the left. Listen for the whistle of the "rock rabbits", more correctly called pikas, on the rockfield. Turn right onto the Timberline Trail.

The Timberline Trail begins to drop gently, passes two shallow lakes, and goes in and out of stands of trees and over small streams lined with extravagant displays of wildflowers. The gentians are particularly spectacular later in the summer. The trail turns away from the mountain, follows a ridge leaving the glorious wildflowers and views of the mountain and canyons, and enters the forest. As you walk along the ridge, take the time to turn around to enjoy the dramatic views of Mt Hood.

The rest of the hike in in beautiful forest. Pass the McGee Creek Trail #627 on the right, and continue to a 4-way intersection, about one mile after the trail enters the forest. Take the right fork, now the Pacific Crest Trail. Stay on the Pacific Crest Trail for only about 50 yards to a fork. Take the left fork, Top

Spur Trail (#784A), for ½ mile through beautiful open forest to the trailhead. The beargrass is this section of the forest is particularly spectacular in a good beargrass year.

McNEIL POINT: For those who want more challenge and more elevation gain, and are willing to forego some of the extravagant displays of flowers on the segment of the Timberline Trail included in this hike, the steep climb up to the McNeil Point Shelter offers an attractive alternative route.

It is sometimes hard to find the takeoff for this trail, but if you follow the instructions for the clockwise route and the map, you should be able to find it without too much difficulty. The trail climbs steadily for about 700 ft. to the shelter. It is quite faint in places but you can usually see where it is going. The last part is quite a scramble, but is not dangerous or particularly scary. Either return back the same way to the Timberline Trail or find the *high* trail that will take you back to the Timberline Trail, initially along the same contour as the shelter. There is often snow up here until late July and care may be needed when crossing the snowfields. The trail curves around and drops into an exquisite little valley with a beautiful flower-lined stream and alpine meadow. When the trail joins the main Timberline Trail, turn *left* and follow the Timberline Trail for a short distance to the junction of the Mazama Trail, on the right. When you turn onto the Mazama Trail you are leaving the Timberline Trail.

McNeil Point *is named after Fred McNeil, a news reporter and editor for almost 45 years, and tireless hiker and climber, who was captivated by Mt Hood and wrote the first substantive history of the mountain,* *McNeil's Mount Hood.*

The Mazama Trail is the rebuilt Cathedral Ridge Trail which was closed for several years after being badly damaged during a particularly tempestuous winter. Mazama members and volunteers took 4 years (1992-1996) for the extensive reconstruction; so far, the work has taken a total of 750 person-days.

Rhododendron

SEGMENT FOUR

MAZAMA TRAILHEAD -- VISTA RIDGE TRAILHEAD

*FEATURES: Eden Park is an
exquisite lush meadow; stone shelter
in Cairn Basin; magnificent views
of the north side of Mt. Hood, with
folded glaciers and precipitous slopes.*

DIFFICULTY: **Strenuous**; long access trails.

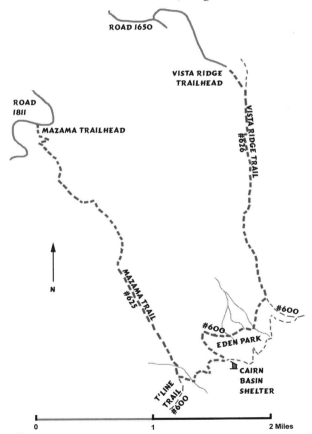

50

DISTANCE: 8.0 miles one way
Elevation Gain : 2700 ft. if hiked clockwise from
Mazama Trailhead, 1800 ft. if hiked
counterclockwise from Vista Ridge Trailhead.

MAPS:
Mt Hood Wilderness Map;
Green Trails: Gov't Camp#461, Hood River#430;
USGS: Mt Hood North, Bull Run Lake

DESCRIPTION: This segment provides a good
workout with fairly long access trails and a relatively
short (2.2 mile) segment on the Timberline Trail.
The rewards are the delightful Cairn Basin and
Eden Park, with their extravagant displays of wild
flowers and magnificent views of the imposing
north face of Mt Hood with its folded glaciers and
precipitous slopes. As with all of the segments,
don't expect to whizz through the meadows and
forested areas. The views are so striking, the flowers
so prolific, and the streams so enchanting that even
the most jaded person finds reason to linger at one
of these magical places.

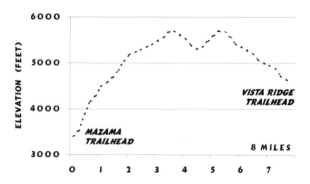

There is an option of taking a high trail to or from
Cairn Basin. This option will cut off 0.4 mile, keep
you on a higher contour, and avoid some of the
elevation gain and loss, but it leaves out Eden Park
which is one of the jewels of the Timberline Trail.

CLOCKWISE OR COUNTERCLOCKWISE?

Both are equally interesting. The Mazama Trail #625 is slightly longer (3.1 miles) and has 500 ft more elevation gain (total 2200 ft) than the Vista Ridge Trail #626 (2.5 miles, 1700 ft), so this may be a consideration.

RIVER CROSSING: There are two easy crossings: a branch of Ladd Creek and a branch of McGee Creek. Neither usually poses a problem.

CAR SHUTTLE OR CAR SWAP: This hike works well as a car swap or car shuttle. The shuttle is a long one, however, so a car swap is certainly appealing. If using a car swap, the more rugged car should be parked at the Vista Ridge Trailhead because the last 0.8 miles of the access road is very rough and rocky. If you are using a car shuttle, remember to take an extra key for the other car in case you manage to miss each other on the trail. This is a potential problem on this trail because there are several side trails in the camping areas in both Eden Park and Cairn Basin.

Avalanche Lilies

TRAILHEADS: If hiking clockwise, park at the Mazama Trailhead; if hiking counterclockwise, park at the Vista Ridge Trailhead. The trailheads can be reached from the Lolo Pass Road, if coming from Hwy 26 (from Portland or the Mt Hood corridor), or from Hood River. Since the approaches are very different when coming from Hwy 26 and the Lolo Pass Road, or from Hood River and Hwy35, the two approaches will be described separately.

If taking Hwy 26 east from Portland, pass through Gresham, Sandy and Wemme and turn left in Zigzag onto the Lolo Pass Road #18. Stay on the Lolo Pass Road for 10.5 miles to the top of Lolo Pass. The paved road ends here. The Mazama Trailhead is 18.5 miles from Hwy 26; the Vista Ridge Trailhead is 21 miles.

To reach the Mazama Trailhead:

Turn right onto Road 1810 just after you reach the top of Lolo Pass. The road becomes good quality gravel. Continue on Road 1810 for 5.4 miles. Turn right onto Road 1811 and drive another 2.4 miles, still on good gravel road. There is ample parking beside the road.

To reach the Vista Ridge Trailhead:

There are two options for the next section of the highway: straight ahead on Road 18 at the top of Lolo Pass, or to the right at the top of the pass on Road 1810. Road 1810 is twice as long but a little easier on the car; Road 18 is half the distance but definitely rough. Neither posed a major problem for passenger cars in the summer of 1996, but road conditions tend to be quite variable depending on winter damage and budgets available for repairs. If taking Road 18, continue straight at the top of Lolo Pass for 3.3 miles, crossing two trestle bridges after 2.7 miles, and turn onto Road 16, signed to Vista Ridge 8 miles. The road is still good quality gravel.

After 5 miles, the road forks at a wide curve. Take the right fork, Road 1650, signed Blue Ridge Road, and follow it for 2.8 miles to a Y-junction. Take the left fork, signed to Vista Ridge. The road soon deteriorates and the last 0.8 miles to the parking lot is very rough and rocky. Don't despair, however, because the rough road ends in a welcome spacious parking lot.

If taking I-84, take the West Hood River exit 62, continue for 1.1 miles, turn right on 13th Street, and follow signs for Odell. After 8 miles, cross a bridge, turn right, and continue straight at a Y-junction for another 4 miles to a fork. Take the right fork to Dee, and follow signs to Lost Lake. Continue, now on Road 13, through Dee, to the junctions of Roads 13 and 18, another 8 miles. Take the left fork, now on Hwy 18.

To reach the Mazama Trailhead:
Continue on Road 18 for 8.5 miles, turn left on Road 1810 and turn left again on Road 1811. The Mazama Trail parking area is another 2.4 miles, still on a good quality road. There is ample parking.

Avalanche Lilies

To reach the Vista Ridge Trailhead:
Continue on Road 18 for 3.4 miles, turn left on
Road 16 and right on Road 1650, signed to Blue
Ridge Road. Follow this for 2.5 miles to a Y-
junction, and take the left fork, signed to Vista
Ridge. The road soon deteriorates and the last 0.8
miles before the parking area is very rough and
rocky. Don't despair, however, because the rough
road ends in a welcome, spacious parking area.

CLOCKWISE: *MAZAMA TRAILHEAD TO VISTA RIDGE TRAILHEAD:*

Remember to sign in at the Wilderness Permit Box

The trail starts at the parking lot
and almost immediately starts to
climb steeply, initially zigzagging
up a rock field, then continuing
to zigzag up to the crest of
Cathedral Ridge through a
hillside of rhododendron
bushes. This part of the trail was
completely rebuilt by the
Mazamas after it was badly
damaged in the mid 1980s. The
trail continues through the
forest and up along Cathedral
Ridge. Stretches with steeper
slopes are interspersed with

White Hellebore

more gentle stretches and shady forest alternates
with more open forest. The undergrowth up the
ridge is brushy with rhododendrons, huckleberry,
some chinquapin, and luxurious beargrass. The
beargrass only flowers well in the less shady
sections.

Continue climbing steadily for about two miles
before the first dramatic views of the mountain
appear directly ahead. Over the next mile, the

mountain comes steadily closer and more imposing. The last stretch before emerging just below the Timberline Trail is in the forest, along the side of a ridge with a steep drop off on the right, then beside a rock field on the left. Watch and listen for the peeps of the "rock rabbits", more correctly called pikas.

Turn left onto the Timberline Trail. This next section of the Timberline Trail has a lot of traffic, mostly from day hikers coming up from Top Spur or McGee Creek Trailheads. There is good reason for this: this is a gorgeous section of open meadow. A short distance from the junction of the Mazama and Timberline Trails, the trail forks. The left fork is the continuation of the Timberline Trail; the right fork follows up along an exquisite stream, lined with flowers, climbs a steep ridge, and loops back to the west and up to McNeil Point.

> *The Mazamas* was organized on the summit of Mt Hood on July 19, 1894. One party climbed from Cloud Cap on the north side, but most toiled up from Portland and Government Camp. The weather was most inhospitable that day, with thunder and sleet, and a hundred climbers turned back. 155 men and 38 women made it to the top and the Mazamas was born.

Wood
Sorrel

The stream is a perfect place to linger, picnic and enjoy the beauty. Continue along the Timberline Trail, heading clockwise (northeast) over a ridge and cross a fairly vigorous but narrow branch of McGee Creek.

The next trail intersection comes shortly, in Cairn Basin. There is the option here of staying on the main trail (left fork) or taking the higher trail. The main trail dips into Eden Park and then climbs again; the higher trail stays at about the same contour before dropping back to the main trail, and is a bit shorter. If you take the higher trail be sure to turn *left* when you rejoin the Timberline Trail.

Summit Climb, July 1894
The birth of the Mazamas

The dip in and out of Eden Park is strongly recommended. This really is an exquisite bowl with abundant wild flowers and a beautiful, lush meadow. The trail breaks up into a network of social trails radiating from a fairly large camping area at the east end of Eden Park. Try to stay on the main trail which goes down to an easy

crossing of a branch of Ladd Creek. The next section winds through forest interspersed with magical meadows. The next intersection is the Vista Ridge Trail and is quite obvious. Turn left onto the Vista Ridge Trail.

The Vista Ridge Trailhead is 2.5 miles and 1700 ft down a relatively gentle grade. The trail divides just before the parking area: take the left fork to go to the parking area; the continuation of the trail is signed to Red Hill Road.

COUNTERCLOCKWISE: *VISTA RIDGE TRAILHEAD TO MAZAMA TRAILHEAD*

The trail takes off from the end of the parking lot and heads upward at a very gentle grade through young hemlock and into cool shady mature forest with moss-festooned trees.

Remember to sign in at the Wilderness Permit Box

There is a rich undergrowth of huckleberries, beargrass, some rhododendrons and moss-covered rocks. A few mushrooms can be seen in the late summer. Almost immediately, the trail comes to a T-junction: the left fork goes to Red Hill Road 1½ miles, the right to Timberline Trail 2½ miles. Foot traffic only.

The trail heads up Vista Ridge through open forest, again with plentiful underbrush of huckleberries, mountain azaleas, a few rhododendrons, beargrass and glades of avalanche lilies in the more open meadow areas. Views of rolling, forested ridges appear to the left as it becomes more obvious that the trail is ascending a ridge.

The open areas become more frequent and drier and the trees more stunted. The flowers change, too, with lupines, partridge foot, paintbrush, pasque flower and heather appearing. Later in the summer, the scarlet berries of the mountain ash provide a slash of color. To the left, views of Mt Hood Village on Hwy 35 appear through the trees and Mt Adams and the eastern plateau of the Columbia Gorge can be seen in the distance. Mt Hood suddenly appears ahead and soon the trail joins the Timberline Trail at a T-junction, signed to Elk Cove (left) and Eden Park to the right.

Western Pasque Flower

*Western Pasque
Flower's Fruit
(Old Man of the Mountain)*

Take the right fork, now on the Timberline Trail, heading down through shady forest and into a meadow. Lost Lake can be seen to the north. The view of Mt Hood is lost for a while as the trail winds through sections of forest interspersed with magical meadows.

The trail crosses a stream and dips down over a narrow branch of Ladd Creek which is usually very easy to cross.

It may be a bit hard to find the continuation of the trail because there are many crossing sites and social trails on the far bank, mostly leading to a fairly large camping area at the east end of Eden Park.

The Timberline Trail can be picked up on the far right of the campsite. The trail then makes a wide loop around Eden Park, climbs up the hillside on the far side, and loops back overlooking the meadow with spectacular views to the north of Mts Rainier, St Helens, and Adams.

The trail switchbacks up the hillside and into Cairn Basin. At a Y-junction, take the right fork; the left is an alternative high trail back to the east. Continue on the trail for a further 0.7 miles, crossing a vigorous, but fairly narrow branch of McGee Creek and up and over the last ridge before a wide open meadow. The trail branches here with the left branch going up beside a creek and eventually over to McNeil Point. The right branch continues on the Timberline Trail and very soon comes to a well-marked fork. The right fork is the Mazama Trail (#625). Follow the Mazama Trail down Cathedral Ridge for 3.1 miles to the parking area.

The last mile is a steep series of switchbacks, first through the forest, then across an impressive rock field. This is the new section of the trail built by the Mazamas and volunteers between 1992-96.

Stone Shelter in Cairn Basin

SEGMENT FIVE

VISTA RIDGE TRAILHEAD - CLOUD CAP

FEATURES: Elk Cove, under Coe Glacier, is one of the loveliest spots on the Timberline Trail: breathtaking meadows and whole hillsides alive and ablaze with beargrass, Indian paintbrush, and lupines; glades white with avalanche lilies; dramatic Eliot and Coe Glaciers.

Historic Cloud Cap

DIFFICULTY: **Strenuous**
distance, elevation gain, two river crossings

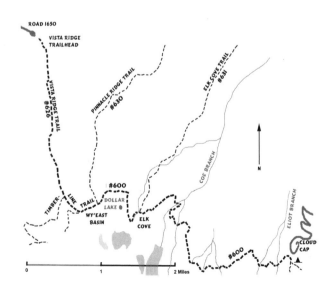

DISTANCE: 9.4 miles one way
Elevation Gain: 2440 ft. if hiked clockwise from
Vista Ridge Trailhead, **1060 ft**.if hiked
counterclockwise from Cloud Cap

MAPS:
Mt Hood Wilderness Map;
Green Trails, Mt Hood #462;
USGS Mt Hood North

DESCRIPTION: This is one of the most dramatic
and favorite segments of the Timberline Trail. Most
people hike this section as a day hike from Cloud
Cap, making peaceful Elk Cove their turn-around
point. Doing this section as a car swap has the
advantage of not having to retrace your steps in and
out of the Coe River canyon. This segment has
incredible views of the Eliot and Coe glaciers and
sometimes challenging river crossings (when they
are still covered with snow bridges). Overall, this
segment arguably has the most sensational displays
of wildflowers of any on the Timberline Trail,
though admittedly this is a hard call because several
of the other segments would come a close second.

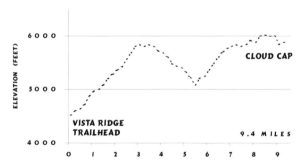

CLOCKWISE OR COUNTERCLOCKWISE?
Fortunately, there isn't much to choose between the
two directions, so both participants in a car swap
will come out equally well. There is about 1300 ft
more elevation gain when hiking clockwise (from

Vista Ridge to Cloud Cap) because of the access up the Vista Ridge Trail. The grade is very easy, however, and the trail has some very dramatic viewpoints that are more likely to be missed when hiking down Vista Ridge.

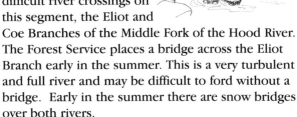

RIVER CROSSINGS:

There are two potentially difficult river crossings on this segment, the Eliot and Coe Branches of the Middle Fork of the Hood River. The Forest Service places a bridge across the Eliot Branch early in the summer. This is a very turbulent and full river and may be difficult to ford without a bridge. Early in the summer there are snow bridges over both rivers.

Take great care when crossing a snow bridge! Don't do this if you are alone! If there isn't a bridge, or snow bridge, it is probably best to go upstream until you can find a spot where the river isn't too turbulent.

CAR SWAP OR CAR SHUTTLE: A car swap works better than a shuttle because the shuttle is very long, although by no means impossible. A shuttle will add about 1½ hours at both ends of the day. If doing a car swap, the more rugged car should probably be left at the Vista Ridge Trailhead because the last 0.8 mile of the access road is very rough and

Cloud Cap

rocky. Remember to take a spare car key for the other car in case you manage to miss each other on the trail.

TRAILHEADS: If hiking clockwise, park at the Vista Ridge Trailhead; if hiking counterclockwise, park at Cloud Cap.

The trailheads to this segment of the Timberline Trail are both on the north side of the mountain and getting there entails a relatively long drive. Also, the access roads to the trailheads may be rough. This will depend on the

Mountain Ash

amount of maintenance that has been done after the winter, whether the access roads have had a major regrading, and for the Cloud Cap road, the amount of car traffic over the summer. The road to Cloud Cap usually has rough sections with some potholes and washboard surface, but these don't pose a serious problem if you drive cautiously. The access road to the Vista Ridge Trailhead is usually fine up to the last 0.8 mile when it deteriorates to being rough and very rocky. Fortunately this section is not long and if it is too difficult, the length of the hike is only increased a little. These comments about the access roads are not intended to scare anyone off, but to provide a realistic description of the access to the trailheads. The hike is overwhelmingly worth the minor inconvenience of the drive. Also, conditions will change from year to year. If in doubt about the roads, as for all of the hikes in this book, call the Forest Service for an up-to-date report. The Vista Ridge Trailhead is 21.8 miles from Hwy 26, and 32 miles from I-84. Cloud Cap is 13 miles from Hwy 35.

If taking Hwy 26 from Portland, pass through Gresham, Sandy, and Wemme to ZigZag. Then...

To reach the Vista Ridge Trailhead: Turn left off Hwy 26 in Zigzag onto the Lolo Pass Road 18. Continue to the top of Lolo Pass, 10.5 miles from Hwy 26. From the top of Lolo Pass, there are two options for the next section: straight ahead on Road 18, or to the right on Road 1810. Road 1810 is twice as long but a little easier on the car (note: road conditions will change from year to year). Road 18 is easily passable, however, for passenger cars. If taking Road 18, continue straight at the top of Lolo Pass for 3.3 miles, crossing two trestle bridges after 2.7 miles, and turn onto Road 16 (good quality gravel), signed to Vista Ridge 8 miles. After 5 miles, the road forks at a wide curve. Take the right fork, Blue Ridge Road 1650, and follow it for 2.8 miles to a Y-junction. Take the left fork, signed to Vista Ridge. The road soon deteriorates and the last 0.8 miles is very rough and rocky. Don't despair, however, because the rough road ends in a welcome and spacious parking area.

To reach Cloud Cap: continue on Hwy 26 through Zigzag, Rhododendron and Government Camp and at the junction of Hwys 26 and 35, take Hwy 35 north towards Hood River. Continue north on Hwy 35 for 17 miles from the junction with Hwy 26 and turn left at the sign for the Cooper Spur Ski Area, now on the Cooper Spur Road. Stay on the Cooper Spur Road for 2.5 miles to the Inn at Cooper Spur then turn left and follow the signs to Cooper Spur Ski Area and Tilly Jane Campground. Keep right at the Y-junction after a further 1.5 miles, now on an unpaved road. The road zigzags up to Cloud Cap for another 9 miles; keep right at the junction at 8.4 miles.

If taking I-84:

To reach the Vista Ridge Trailhead: Take the West Hood River exit 62, continue for 1.1 miles, turn right on 13th street and follow signs for Odell. After 8 miles, cross a bridge, turn right, and continue straight at a Y-junction for another 4 miles to a fork. Take the right fork to Dee, and follow signs to Lost Lake. Continue, now on Road 13, through Dee, to the junctions of Roads 13 and 18, another 8 miles. Take the left fork, now on Road 18. Continue on Road 18 for 3.4 miles, turn left on Road 16 and right on Road 1650, signed to Blue Ridge Road. Follow this for 2.5 miles to a Y-junction, and take the left fork, signed to Vista Ridge. The road soon deteriorates and the last 0.8 miles before the parking area is very rough and rocky. Don't despair, however, because the rough road ends in a welcome, spacious parking area.

To reach Cloud Cap: Take the Hwy 35 exit South, drive for 23.5 miles and turn right (west) at the Cooper Spur Ski Area sign, now on the Cooper Spur Road. Stay on the Cooper Spur Road for 2.5 miles to the Inn at Cooper Spur then turn left and follow the signs to Cooper Spur Ski Area and Tilly Jane Campground. Keep right at the Y-junction after a further 1.5 miles, now on an unpaved road. The road zigzags up to Cloud Cap for another 9 miles; keep right at the junction at 8.4 miles.

Partridge Foot

CLOCKWISE: *VISTA RIDGE TRAILHEAD TO CLOUD CAP*

The trail takes off from the end of the parking lot and heads upward at a very gentle grade through young hemlock then into cool shady mature forest with moss-festooned trees.

Remember to sign in at the Wilderness Permit Box.

There is a rich undergrowth of huckleberries, beargrass, some rhododendrons and moss-covered rocks. A few mushrooms can be seen in the late summer. Almost immediately, the trail comes to a T-junction: the left fork goes to Red Hill Road 1½ miles, the right to Timberline Trail 2½ miles. Foot traffic only.

The trail heads up Vista Ridge through open forest, again with plentiful underbrush of huckleberries, mountain azaleas, a few rhododendrons, beargrass and glades of avalanche lilies in the more open meadow areas. Views of rolling, forested ridges appear to the left as it becomes more obvious that the trail is following up a ridge. The open areas

Lunch in Elk Cove

become more frequent and drier and the trees more stunted. The flowers change, too, with lupines, partridge foot, paintbrush, pasque flower and heather appearing. Later in the summer, the scarlet berries of the mountain ash provide a slash of color. To the left, views of Mt Hood Village on Hwy 35 appear through the trees and Mt Adams and the eastern plateau of the Columbia Gorge can be seen in the distance. Mt Hood suddenly appears ahead and soon the trail joins the Timberline Trail at a T-junction.

Turn left, now on the Timberline Trail, and continue through a heath-like area with mountain hemlock and heather, then a lush, marshy meadow, Wy'East Basin. There is a trail intersection, almost immediately: The right fork is the high trail that loops back east to Cairn Basin; the main trail is straight ahead. The trail meanders through beautiful meadows with flower-lined streams and stands of trees.

The next trail intersection, after about ½ mile, is the Pinnacle Ridge Trail on the left (another option for accessing the Timberline Trail). About 1/3 mile from the intersection of the Pinnacle Ridge trail with the Timberline Trail, a faint, unmarked trail to Dollar Lake takes off to the right. This is a delightful, and well worthwhile, 0.2 mile side trip if time and energy levels allow (see optional add-on, below). Continue for a short distance along the side of the ridge that borders Elk Cove, and drop down into the beautiful cove.

The Elk Cove Trail intersects with the main Timberline Trail about the middle of the cove, after the stream (the Elk Cove Trail is another option for accessing the Timberline Trail). Continue on through Elk Cove and down into the canyon carved by the Coe Branch of the Middle Fork of the Hood

River coming down from the Coe glacier. Crossing this may be a challenge early in the summer when there are still snow bridges over the rivers. Later in the year, it is usually quite easy. The trail climbs out of the canyon in long loops, following an easy grade.

The next 3 miles are relatively easy as the trail follows the contours of the mountain at more or less the same elevation. The stream crossings are easy. The next challenge is crossing the Eliot Branch of the Middle Fork of the Hood River. There is usually a sturdy bridge over the river, put in place by the Forest Service each summer. If you are crossing before the bridge is placed, take great care, especially

Avalanche Lily

on the snow bridges. After crossing the river, there is only one short uphill stretch before the Cloud Cap Trailhead, campground and parking area.

COUNTERCLOCKWISE: CLOUD CAP TRAILHEAD TO VISTA RIDGE TRAILHEAD

The Timberline Trail skirts the campground and is clearly signed by a noticeboard.

Remember to sign in at the Wilderness Permit Box.

Take the trail to the right, signed to Elk Cove. The trail almost immediately starts to go downhill into the canyon carved by the Eliot Branch of the Middle Fork of the Hood River. The Forest Service puts a bridge over the river every summer but if you are there before the bridge, take great care crossing, especially on the snow bridges, because the river is very turbulent and usually very full. The next three miles of the trail are relatively easy because the trail meanders along through meadows and stands of trees, mostly following the contours of the mountain, and doesn't gain or lose much elevation. There are fairly steep drop-offs on the right in some places, though, so take care not to miss your footing. The next notable landmark is the canyon of the Coe Branch of the Middle Fork of the Hood River. The trail eases down to the river by way of long loops at a very gentle grade. This river does not have a bridge and, again, special care is needed early in the summer. Later, there is usually no problem.

After crossing the Coe Branch, the trail climbs out of the canyon and into Elk Cove, another 1¼ miles. Elk Cove is a great place to picnic, rest, look at flowers or gaze at the awesome folds of the Coe Glacier. The mountain is so close at this point that is seems that a mere hop, skip, and jump would get you to the top. Wrong! Continue on through Elk Cove, cross the exquisite stream that runs through the west side of the cove, and follow the trail up and over the ridge that forms the west side of the cove. The display of flowers on this stretch is equal to any other segment on the Timberline Trail, which is saying a lot! Once out of Elk Cove, the trail continues to follow more or less the same contour and passes through lovely meadows and stands of trees. For a well worthwhile side trip to Dollar Lake (see below), take an unmarked trail on the left after the climb out from Elk Cove where the mountain comes into view on the left. The next trail intersection is Pinnacle Ridge, on the right, in a meadow.

The Vista Ridge Trail is 0.6 miles further, on the far side of the lush Wy'East Basin. Turn right down Vista Ridge Trail for the last 2.7 miles to the trailhead. The trail follows the ridge all the way and descends at a gentle grade. Take the time to stop at some of the fantastic viewpoints looking back up to the mountain.There is only one more intersection, ½ mile from the trailhead: turn left to get to the trailhead; straight ahead goes to Red Hills Road, 1½ miles.

OPTIONAL ADD-ON: The short (0.2 mile) hike up to Dollar Lake, and to the view points beyond, is well worth the effort because it provides superb views down into Elk Cove and up to the Coe Glacier and Barrett Spur. Dollar Lake is a very shallow mountain tarn, not suitable for swimming or fishing, but perfect for a picnic, a quiet nap, or overnight camping.

Wild Strawberry

Cloud Cap Inn was built by Chinese laborers and opened in August 1889 at a cost of over $50,000. The hoped-for guests did not materialize, and the Inn had to be closed at the end of the 1890 season, after only two years in operation. Perhaps the length of the journey was in part responsible. Visitors would travel from Portland to Hood River by train and be met by an open coach and four. The first relay was 10 miles to the Joe Divers Ranch on the Little Luckamas Creek. The second relay took them to the Elk Creek; the third up the long dusty road to Cloud Cap—5½ to 6 hours from the railway. Cloud Cap is now operated by the Crag Rats, a mountain rescue group.

Women on Mt. Hood

Fanny Case   *Mary Robinson*

"A party of gentlemen and ladies from Salem and vicinity has just returned from a trip to Mt Hood, and Mr John Garrison, of the party, called upon us yesterday morning. He reports that on last Monday, Aug 26, 1867, several gentlemen and two ladies made the ascent to the summit, starting from the snowline at seven a.m. and reaching the summit at ten minutes past one p.m. They remained one hour on the summit, left several mementoes of their visit and descended again to the camp of the night before, arriving at five minutes past five o'clock.

"The names of the ladies are Miss Fanny S.Case and Miss Mary Robinson both of Salem. Mr Garrison says they exhibited remarkable courage and endurance, making the trip without difficulty and visiting all the notable points to which the gentlemen ventured. This achievement is something for them to boast of, as they are absolutely the first white women who ever stood on the summit of Mt Hood. The late ascent by ladies of Mt Adams dwindles into insignificance compared with it. Henceforth Miss Case and Miss Robinson are entitled to the first distinction as female adventurers."

Daily Oregonian Aug 31, 1867

Eliot Glacier was named after Dr Thomas Eliot, a Portland Unitarian minister, who explored the north side of Mt Hood and found, and named, Lost Lake.

Coe Glacier was named after Captain Henry Coe who explored the north-east part of Mt Hood in 1883 with the idea of establishing a tourist resort.

SEGMENT SIX

CLOUD CAP -- SAHALIE FALLS TRAILHEAD

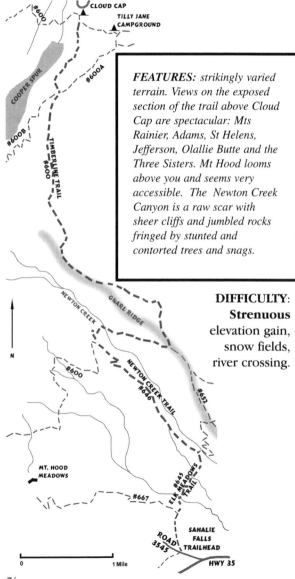

FEATURES: *strikingly varied terrain. Views on the exposed section of the trail above Cloud Cap are spectacular: Mts Rainier, Adams, St Helens, Jefferson, Olallie Butte and the Three Sisters. Mt Hood looms above you and seems very accessible. The Newton Creek Canyon is a raw scar with sheer cliffs and jumbled rocks fringed by stunted and contorted trees and snags.*

DIFFICULTY:
Strenuous
elevation gain,
snow fields,
river crossing.

DISTANCE: 8.3 miles one way
Elevation Gain: 1650 ft. if hiked from Cloud Cap,
2990 ft. if hiked from Sahalie Falls Trailhead

MAPS:
Mt Hood Wilderness Map;
Green Trails, Mt Hood #462; USGS Mt Hood North
& South Quadrangles

DESCRIPTION: This section of the Timberline trail climbs to the highest and most exposed point of the trail (7350 ft), and crosses Newton Creek. There are likely to be large patches of snow to cross, even in August and September, but these are not usually a problem because the pitch of the snow fields is not steep. The elevation and exposure make this section very different from most of the others. Instead of meadows of flowers, there are stunted pines contorted into weird shapes and stunted alpine flowers carpeting the rocky face of the mountain. The views in every direction are spectacular. The height, views and openness of the terrain easily lead to the illusion that you can fly without any effort. The Newton Creek crossing poses some challenge but is no more difficult than most of the other river crossings.

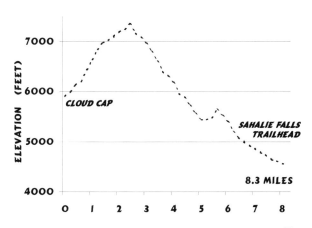

The flowers on this hike also vary according to the section and the terrain. On the exposed and high part, there are plentiful flowers, but they are all dwarfed by the extreme conditions. Look for large patches of stonecrop, pussy paws, phlox and dwarfed lupines. Beside the streams, look for monkey flowers, penstemon, gentians and Jacob's Ladder. In the areas around the timber line, look for cat's ears, fleabane, carpets of lupine and beautiful grasses. The section between the Sahalie Falls Trailhead and the Timberline Trail is through shady forest with huckleberry bushes and low shrubs, bunchberry, wild strawberries and pipsissewa, with lots of beargrass early in the summer in a good year.

CLOCKWISE OR COUNTERCLOCKWISE?
The clockwise direction (Cloud Cap to Sahalie Falls Trailhead) is definitely easier with appreciably less elevation gain (1650 ft vs 2990 ft). The clockwise direction starts at about the timber line, crosses the exposed section of Mt Hood at the beginning, and has the river crossing about ¾ way through the hike. The counterclockwise direction feels more of an achievement because the hike starts in the forest and climbs steadily for almost six miles; the river crossing comes earlier in the hike. If there are doubts about the weather closing in, it might be a good idea to go clockwise and cover the exposed section at the beginning of the hike.

Crossing Newton Creek

RIVER CROSSING: There is one river crossing in Newton Canyon. As with all of the river crossings on the Timberline Trail, the amount of water, and therefore the difficulty, can vary appreciably depending on the snow melt and time of day. This crossing can vary from being quite difficult to being relatively easy. On the plus side, the river isn't very deep or turbulent and there are plenty of rocks to hold on to.

CAR SHUTTLE OR CAR SWAP: This hike works well with a car shuttle or car swap. The shuttle is a long one (30 miles, 1 hour each way), but is not hard. Remember to take a spare key for the other car, if doing a car swap, in case you manage to miss each other on the trail.

TRAILHEADS: If hiking clockwise, start from the Cloud Cap Trailhead; if hiking counterclockwise, start from the Sahalie Falls Trailhead. Both trailheads are reached from Hwy 35, the Mt Hood loop highway. To reach Hwy 35, either take Hwy 26 east to Government Camp, then Hwy 35 north towards Hood River, or drive east on I-84 to Hood River and take the Hwy 35 exit south. The road up to Cloud Cap may vary from slow, but quite reasonable, to very slow with potholes (later in the summer) and sections of bad washboard surface, depending on the traffic and the budget for maintenance. If doing a car swap, the sturdier car should go up to Cloud Cap because the road becomes rutted with heavy traffic during the summer. To reach Cloud Cap it takes about the same driving time to go up the Columbia Gorge on I-84, as it takes to drive east on Hwy 26. Both are very scenic drives. The Gorge route has more freeway driving. The Sahalie Falls Trailhead can also be reached by either route, but the route through Government Camp is definitely shorter.

If driving east on Hwy 26 from Portland, pass through Gresham, Sandy, Wemme, Zigzag, Rhododendron and Government Camp. 2.2 miles after Government Camp, at the junction with Hwy 35, take the right fork and continue north towards Hood River, now on Hwy 35.

To reach Cloud Cap: Continue north on Hwy 35 for 17 miles from the junction with Hwy 26 and turn left at the sign for the Cooper Spur Ski Area, now on the Cooper Spur Road. Stay on the Cooper Spur Road for 2.4 miles to the Inn at Cooper Spur then turn left and follow the signs to Cooper Spur Ski Area and Tilly Jane Campground. Keep right at the Y-junction after a further 1.5 miles, now on an unpaved road. The road zigzags up to Cloud Cap for another 9 miles; keep right at the junction at 8.4 miles.

To reach the Sahalie Falls Trailhead: Turn left at the sign for the Mt Hood Nordic Center, 7.9 miles from the junction with Hwy 26, now on Road 3545. The Sahalie Falls Trailhead is 0.4 miles further, on the right, and is signed to Umbrella Falls and Elk Meadows Trail.

If taking I-84, take the Hwy 35 exit in Hood River and drive south.

To reach Cloud Cap: Take Hwy 35 south and turn right onto Cooper Spur Road at the Cooper Spur and Tilly Jane Campground sign, 23.5 miles from Hood River. After 2.5 miles, turn left following the signs to Cooper Spur Ski Area and Tilly Jane Recreational Area. Keep right at the Y- junction after a further 1.5 miles, now on an unpaved road. The road zigzags up to Cloud Cap for another 9 miles; keep right at the junction at 8.4 miles.

To reach the Sahalie Falls Trailhead: Take Hwy 35 south and turn right 32 miles from the junction with I-84. The Sahalie Falls Trailhead is 0.4 miles further on the right, and is signed to Umbrella Falls and Elk Meadows Trail.

CLOCKWISE: *CLOUD CAP TO SAHALIE FALLS TRAILHEAD*

The trail starts towards the back of the campground and is signed to Gnarl Ridge.

Remember to sign in at the Wilderness Permit Box.

The trail branches almost immediately; take the left fork and continue to climb gently to the timber line through open meadows. The trail soon clears the treeline, climbs up the side of a gulley, crosses small streams, and heads steadily upwards onto the exposed flank of Mt Hood. Stone cairns mark the trail so it is easy to follow even when it disappears under snow. One mile from Cloud Cap, there is a four-way intersection: the right fork climbs up to Cooper Spur; the left goes to Tilly Jane Campground. Keep straight on, continuing to climb gently to the highest point of the trail, 7350 ft. At this point it feels as if you are under the armpit of Mt Hood. If it is sunny and clear, the feeling of height is heady; if it is cloudy, misty or raining, it can feel very eerie. The wind is seldom absent and the sulphurous smell from the vents on the mountain add to the feeling of mystery.

Once past the highest point, the trail heads down towards Gnarl Ridge and the Newton Creek Canyon. Here, the views change again with the dramatic canyon walls in the fore.

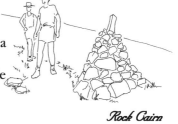

The trail follows the rim of the canyon for a short distance, then curves around the side of Gnarl Ridge and Lambertson Butte, now well below the

Rock Cairn

canyon rim. Continue downwards through open forest to a 3-way intersection: the Timberline Trail is the right fork; straight ahead is the Gnarl Ridge Trail #652 to Elk Meadows.

Take the right fork which continues down through the trees into Newton Canyon. Cross Newton Creek and find the continuation of the trail almost hidden in the bushes. The trail climbs out of the canyon at a gentle grade. Just at a right hand turn, the trail divides. The Timberline Trail heads off to the right. Take the left fork, signed Newton Creek Trail # 646, and follow this gently downhill, parallel to Newton Creek, for 2 miles to a T- junction with the Elk Meadows Trail # 645. Take the right fork and continue for a further 1 mile, crossing Clark Creek on a sturdy bridge. After Clark Creek, follow the signs for the Sahalie Falls Trailhead, passing trails to the Elk Meadows trailhead on the left and Umbrella Falls on the right.

Crossing a Snowfield

COUNTERCLOCKWISE: *SAHALIE FALLS TRAILHEAD TO CLOUD CAP*

Be sure to take the trail on the *right* side of the road, signed to Umbrella Falls Trail and Elk Meadows Trail. At ¼ mile the trail meets the old trail from the Nordic Center. Keep right and continue for about ¾ mile, passing the trail to Umbrella Falls (#667) on the left and a little later, the east end of the Elk Meadows Trail on the right.

Remember to sign in at the Wilderness Permit Box.

Snag on Gnarl Ridge

Continue straight at this intersection on the Elk Meadows Trail (# 645) and cross Clark Creek on a sturdy bridge. The Newton Creek Trail (#646) junction is about ½ mile after the bridge, on the left.

Turn left onto Newton Creek Trail and climb gently for 2 miles through shady forest, parallel to Newton Creek. This is not one of the trails that is well maintained, so expect some natural hazards, such as small trees down across the trail. These do not create a problem, however. The last section of the trail, before it reaches the Timberline Trail, climbs more steeply in long zigzags. At the T-junction with the Timberline Trail (#600), take the right fork.

The Timberline Trail immediately drops down into Newton Creek Canyon. Cross the river and climb back out of the canyon. At a 3-way intersection once you have climbed out of the canyon, take the left fork—the right is the Gnarl Ridge Trail #652. Continue to climb at a fairly gentle grade through open forest and meadows, curve around the far side of Lambertson Butte and up to narrow Gnarl Ridge. Views here up to Mt Hood and down into the Newton Creek Canyon are spectacular. The trail runs just below the top of the ridge, then takes off to the right, crosses a snowfield and climbs to the highest point of the trail (7350 ft).

The trail descends gradually to Cloud Cap across the rocky open mountain side, and is well marked by cairns. There is only one more intersection: a four-way intersection with trail #600A&B that goes from Cooper Spur to Tilly Jane Campground. Keep straight at the 4-way intersection for the last 1.1 miles to the Cloud Cap campground and trailhead.

HISTORY OF THE TIMBERLINE TRAIL

August 14, 1854, William Barlow party made the first recorded ascent of Mt Hood.

1892: first recorded circuit of Mt Hood on foot by Will Langille, a climbing guide, and a companion.

1934 - 1938: construction of the Timberline Trail by the Civilian Conservation Corps.

VOLCANIC HISTORY OF MT HOOD

Age: *Late Pleistocene*
Diameter: *7 miles (east-west at 4000ft)*
Volume of cone: *45 cubic miles*
Distance from the Columbia: *22 miles*
Number of glaciers: *11*
Recent eruptions: *1804, 1853, 1854, 1859, 1865, 1907*

Mt Hood is one of a string of volcanoes forming the Cascade Range and stretching from Mt Lassen in California to Mt Garibaldi in British Columbia. The Cascade volcanoes erupt far less frequently than the Hawaiian volcanoes, but their proximity to populated areas make them potentially more dangerous.

The Cascade volcanoes are composite volcanoes, have steep sides, and erupt magma that is very sticky. The expanding gases can't escape easily from the sticky magma and build up pressure, leading to explosive eruptions. The Hawaiian volcanoes are shield volcanoes, so called because their long sloping sides look like an inverted warrior's shield.

The known periods of Mt Hood's active eruptions include a period during the last Ice Age between 12,000 and 25,000 years ago, another period about 1500 years ago, and a third period between 1780 and 1910. Lewis and Clark, in 1805, saw some of the effects of an eruption which was probably in the early 1790s. They described a river (the Sandy) that was essentially choked with sandy sediment, much like the Toutle River after the eruption of Mt St Helens in 1980.

Mt Hood's eruptions have mostly been characterized by lava flows and dome-building and dome-collapsing, rather than very explosive. The most recent period of eruptions was centered at Crater Rock, about 700 ft below the summit, and involved pyroclastic flows of gas, rock and ash, and mudslides primarily involving the mountain's south side.

No one knows when Mt Hood will erupt again, but erupt it will - almost certainly.

SEGMENT SEVEN

SAHALIE FALLS TRAILHEAD -- UMBRELLA FALLS TRAILHEAD

FEATURES: *Flower lovers will find the profusion of flowers on this segment a very pleasant distraction. The mix of flowers will change throughout the summer but the extravagance of the display lasts throughout the season. The many streams crossing the trail are lined with glorious masses of riotous color. Views in every direction are spectacular.*

DIFFICULTY: Moderately Strenuous
modest elevation gain, river crossing

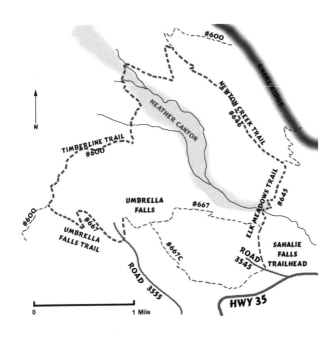

DISTANCE: 7.0 miles one way
Elevation Gain: 1660 ft. if hiked clockwise from
Sahalie Falls, **980 ft.** if hiked from Umbrella Falls
Trailhead

MAPS:
Mt Hood Wilderness Map;
Green Trails, Mt Hood # 462;
USGS Mt Hood South Quadrangle

DESCRIPTION: This section takes the prize for
accessibility, short car shuttle, flexibility (loop
possible), and the extravagant display of flowers. It
is also the easiest section with relatively little
elevation gain. Most of the elevation gain occurs at
the beginning, from the trailhead to the Timberline
Trail. This section of the Timberline Trail crosses Mt
Hood Meadows Ski Area, so much of the trail is on
meadows that are ski runs in winter.

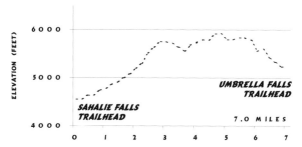

Many small streams cross the trail; each one is lined
with flowers and looks as if it belongs in a Sierra
Club calendar. This section can easily be made into
a loop (see map and directions at the end). A short
side trip to Umbrella Falls is an added bonus. The
list of flowers and shrubs to look for is very long
and includes shooting stars (very early in the
summer), beargrass, lupines, Indian paintbrush,
partridge foot, Pasque flower (first the flower, then
the mop-head of seed pods), pink and yellow
monkeyflowers, penstemon, heather, mountain
spirea, buttercups, fireweed, pipsissewa (in the

shaded areas of the access trails). Later on in the summer, Old Man of the Mountain, asters, goldenrod and mountain ash.

CLOCKWISE OR COUNTERCLOCKWISE?
Both directions are equally interesting once you are on the Timberline Trail. The counterclockwise direction (starting from the Umbella Falls Trailhead) has a shorter access trail to the Timberline Trail (1½ vs 3 miles), slightly less elevation gain, and more flowers on the access trail.

Crossing Clark Creek

RIVER CROSSING: There is one river crossing on the Timberline Trail section, Clark Creek. Somehow the word "creek" doesn't seem appropriate for this, often turbulent, body of water! Sometimes there are sturdy branches laid across the creek, sometimes there aren't. As with all of the river crossings on the Timberline Trail, the amount of water in the river, and therefore the difficulty, can vary appreciably depending on the snow melt and time of day. It can be a tricky crossing when carrying a heavy backpack so, as always, be careful!

Pussy Paws

CAR SHUTTLE OR CAR SWAP:

This hike has by far the shortest car shuttle of all the hikes in this book, and it will only add about 15 minutes to the hike at the beginning and end of the day. Note also that this hike is easily made into a loop by using the Umbrella Falls Trail (see map), so a car shuttle or swap is convenient, but not essential.

Shooting Star

TRAILHEADS: To hike clockwise, start at the Sahalie Falls Trailhead; to hike counterclockwise, start at the Umbrella Falls Trailhead. Both trailheads are accessed from Hwy 35, the Mt Hood loop highway. To reach Hwy 35, either take Hwy 26 east to Government Camp, then Hwy 35 north towards Hood River; or drive east on I-84 to Hood River and take the Hwy 35 exit south. Both are very scenic drives. The Gorge route has more freeway driving, but is appreciably longer.

If taking Hwy 26 east from Portland, pass through Gresham, Sandy, Wemme, Zigzag, Rhododendron and Government Camp. 2.2 miles after Government Camp, at the junction with Hwy 35, take the right fork and continue towards Hood River, now on Hwy 35.

To reach the Sahalie Falls Trailhead:

Turn left at the sign for the Mt Hood Nordic Center 7.9 miles from the junction with Hwy 26, now on Road 3545. The Sahalie Falls Trailhead is 0.4 miles on the right, and is signed to Umbrella Falls and Elk Meadows.

To reach the Umbrella Falls Trailhead:

Continue on Hwy 35 for 6.8 miles and turn left onto the access road to Mt Hood Meadows Ski

Area. The trailhead is another 1.5 miles on the left of the road, and may be hard to spot. Look for the trailhead signs on either side of the road and park on the shoulder.

If taking I-84, take the Hwy 35 exit at Hood River, and drive south.

To reach the Sahalie Falls Trailhead:

Continue south on Hwy 35 for 32 miles and turn right at the sign for the Hood River Nordic Center. The Sahalie Falls Trailhead is 0.4 miles, on the right, and is signed to Umbrella Falls and Elk Meadows Trail.

To reach the Umbrella Falls Trailhead:

Turn right at the sign for Mt Hood Ski Area, 33.3 miles from Hood River. The trailhead is another 1.5 miles on the left of the road, and may be hard to spot. Look for the trailhead signs on either side of the road and park on the shoulder.

Creek near Mt Hood Meadows

CLOCKWISE: *SAHALIE FALLS TRAILHEAD TO UMBRELLA FALLS TRAILHEAD*

Be sure to take the trail on the *right* side of the road, signed to Umbrella Falls Trail and Elk Meadows Trail. At ¼ mile the trail meets the old trail from the Nordic Center. Keep right and continue for about ¾ mile, passing the trail to Umbrella Falls (#667) on the left and a little later, the east end of the Elk Meadows Trail on the right.

Remember to sign in at the Wilderness Permit Box

Continue straight at this intersection on the Elk Meadows Trail (#645) and cross Clark Creek on a sturdy bridge. The Newton Creek Trail (#646) junction is about ½ mile after the bridge, on the left. Turn left onto Newton Creek Trail and climb gently for 2 miles through shady forest, parallel to Newton Creek. This is not one of the trails that is well maintained now so expect some natural hazards, such as small trees down across the trail. These do not create a problem, however. The last section of the trail, before it reaches the Timberline Trail, climbs more steeply in long zigzags.

At the T-junction with the Timberline Trail (#600), take the left fork. Now on the Timberline Trail, there are no more decisions to make for the next 3.2 miles, to the fork that will take you back down to the Umbrella Falls Trailhead.

After about 1/3 mile on the Timberline Trail, the trail dips down across the banks of Clark Creek and crosses the creek. The landscape changes dramatically here to a stark moonscape of rock and sand. This crossing can be tricky at times, so take time to pick a good crossing place, and be careful! For the rest of the 3.2 miles, the trail winds gently around the mountain passing through lightly

*Hiking across ski runs at
Mt. Hood Meadows*

forested areas, crossing small streams and passing through lush open meadows that are ski runs for Mt Hood Meadows Ski Area in the winter. Several service roads for the ski area cross the Timberline Trail but ignore these and keep on the well-maintained trail.

There is minimal elevation gain or loss and the hiking is very easy and very beautiful. Be prepared for frequent stops to admire the views or take photos. The only decision that needs to be made is when to turn reluctantly off the Timberline Trail and head down to the car. The well-marked trail junction to the Umbrella Falls Trailhead that signals the end of the Timberline Trail segment comes just after a main service road crosses the trail.

At the Y-junction, take the left fork, signed to Umbrella Falls (#667), and follow it down through beautiful forest and lush meadows to the Umbrella Falls Trailhead on the access road to the Mt Hood Meadows Ski Area. If time permits, the short, ¼ mile hike to Umbrella Falls is well worth the extra 15-30 minutes. Take your camera! The trail to Umbrella Falls picks up on the far side of the Mt Hood Ski Area access road, almost opposite the trailhead that you have just reached.

COUNTERCLOCKWISE: *UMBRELLA FALLS TRAILHEAD TO SAHALIE FALLS TRAILHEAD*

If time permits, a short side trip to Umbrella Falls is well worth it. This will add about an extra 15-30 minutes. To do this, take the Umbrella Falls Trail (#667) on the *right* of the Mt Hood Meadows access road. The falls are about ¼ mile from the road, through a beautiful meadow.

The access trail to the Timberline Trail is the continuation of the Umbrella Falls Trail (#667), and takes off on the *left* of the Mt Hood Meadows access road, almost opposite the short trail to the falls. The trail climbs very gently, passing through beautiful forest and soon coming to open areas where the lupines carpet the meadows. There are occasional glimpses of Mt Hood to the north, and Mt Jefferson to the south. The stream crossings provide a preview of the many stream crossings to come with a profusion of flowers clustering around the bank. The clumps of yellow and pink monkeyflowers are particularly colorful.

Indian Paintbrush

91

The Umbrella Falls Trail meets the Timberline Trail after 1½ miles. Take the right arm (left goes to Timberline Lodge), cross a service road and continue, now on theTimberline Trail.

The Timberline Trail, in this section, meanders along the upper part of the ski area, through meadows that are lush with flowers and grasses, under ski tows, through streams, and sometimes through wooded areas. There is minimal elevation gain or loss and the hiking is very easy. Progress is usually slowed, however, by incredible views: Mt Hood to the north, now very close; the endless rolling foothills around Mt Hood; and Mt Jefferson to the south. After leaving the ski area, the trail dips into Clark Canyon, crosses the river, and climbs the sandy bank on the far side. The landscape changes dramatically at this point from lush meadows and cool forest to a stark moonscape of rock and sand.

You are now in the Wilderness Area. The trail climbs out of the canyon, back into the trees briefly, then round a long curve towards Newton Creek. The turnoff to the trail that leads back down to the trailhead is just before the trail dips down into Newton Creek.

Take the Newton Creek Trail (#646) to the right and follow it down for another 2 miles, mostly parallel to Newton Creek, to the junction with the Elk Meadows Trail. This section of the hike is through cool forest. The trail descends gradually and is easy to follow. This is not one of the trails that is well maintained now so expect some natural hazards, such as small trees down across the trail. These do not create a problem, however.

Shooting Star

Turn right at the junction with the Elk Meadows Trail (#645) and follow the signs for the Sahalie Falls Trailhead, crossing Clark Creek on a sturdy bridge and keeping to the right at the trail junction just after the bridge. The Sahalie Falls Trailhead is about one mile from the junction of the Newton Creek and Elk Meadows trails.

SEGMENT EIGHT

UMBRELLA FALLS TRAILHEAD -- TIMBERLINE LODGE

FEATURES: This bike is hard to top: the views of Mt Hood are breathtaking, the alpine flowers and meadows are gorgeous, and the vistas south, once you are out of the canyon, are spectacular. The broad swath of the White River Canyon is a reminder of the awesome power of Mother Nature. The images of this bike will stay with you for a long time.

DIFFICULTY: Moderately Strenuous
if hiked from Timberline Lodge; **Strenuous** from
Umbrella Falls Trailhead:elevation gain, and
crossing of White River

DISTANCE: 6.0 miles one way
Elevation Gain: 1770 ft. if hiked clockwise from
Umbrella Falls Trailhead, **930 ft.** if hiked
counterclockwise from Timberline Lodge

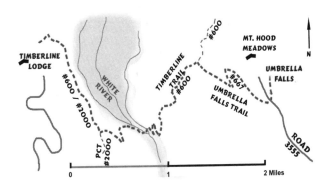

MAPS:
Mt Hood Wilderness Map;
Green Trails, Mt Hood # 462;
USGS Mt Hood South Quadrangle

DESCRIPTION: The last segment of the Timberline Trail when hiking clockwise, the first when hiking counter-clockwise. Since Timberline Lodge is at one end of the hike, almost all of this segment (all but 1½ miles) is on the Timberline Trail. The lowest point of the segment is the impressive White River Canyon, a wide gash of mostly dry river bed that leads from the White River Glacier. The views from this hike are truly spectacular: the shear bulk of Mt Hood is so close that it demands attention; the ghostly snags of dead trees on the ridge to the west of the White River Canyon, the meadows richly carpeted with alpine flowers on the ridge to the east of the canyon; and the endless rolling vistas to the south. The river crossing can be sporting especially when the snow melt is heavy, so care is needed. However, this is usually one of the easiest river crossings on the Timberline Trail.

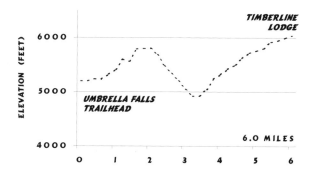

CLOCKWISE OR COUNTERCLOCKWISE?

As can be seen from the elevation map, both directions entail some elevation gain and loss, so it is hard to say which direction poses the greater challenge. Both have their advantages and disadvantages. On a very hot day, the climb from the White River Canyon up to Timberline Lodge can be a real haul, compounded by the softness of the sand on the last stretch of the trail. On the other hand, the views to the south before the descent into the canyon, the views of Mt Hood and the weird shapes of the dead snags on the climb out of the canyon are arguably more impressive when hiking clockwise. The solution is obviously to try both directions and see which you prefer.

RIVER CROSSING: The only river crossing on this segment is the White River. Although the White River Canyon is about 100 yards from bank to bank, the actual river is usually quite narrow and well behaved. The usual care needs to be taken, especially early in the summer, when the river is swollen with snow melt. Take time to find a good place to cross.

CAR SHUTTLE OR CAR SWAP: This hike works well as a car shuttle or car swap. The shuttle is neither long nor difficult and will only add about 40 minutes at the beginning and end of the day. One car should be left at Timberline Lodge, the other at the Umbrella Falls Trailhead on the access road to Mt Hood Meadows Ski Area. Remember to take a spare key for the other car in case you manage to miss each other on the trail.

TRAILHEADS: If hiking clockwise, leave one car at the Umbrella Falls Trailhead; if hiking counterclockwise, park at Timberline Lodge. The Umbrella Falls Trailhead is reached from Hwy 35; Timberline Lodge is accessed from Hwy 26.

Arnica

If taking Hwy 26 east from Portland, pass through Gresham, Sandy, Wemme, Zigzag, Rhododendron, and Government Camp.

To reach the Umbrella Falls Trailhead:

Continue past Government Camp on Hwy 26, heading east, and at the first major junction 2.2 miles past the Summit Rest Area at the far (east) end of the Government Camp Loop, take the Hood River exit which is Hwy 35. Continue on Hwy 35 for 6.8 miles to the Mt Hood Meadows Ski Area access road and turn left onto the access road. The trailhead is another 1½ miles on the left and may be hard to spot. Look for the trailhead signs on either side of the road and park on the shoulder.

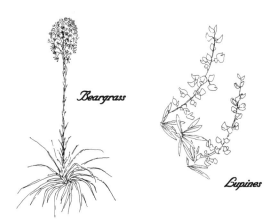

Beargrass

Lupines

To reach Timberline Lodge:

Continue on Hwy 26 past the Summit Rest Area at the far (east) end of the Government Camp loop and turn left (north) onto the Timberline Road just after the Summit Rest Area.

If taking I-84, take the Hwy 35 exit at Hood River, and drive south.

To reach the Umbrella Falls Trailhead:

Drive south on Hwy 35 for 33.3 miles and turn right at the sign for the Mt Hood Meadows Ski Area. The trailhead is another 1½ miles on the left and may be hard to spot. Look for the trailhead signs on either side of the road and park on the shoulder.

To reach Timberline Lodge:

Drive south on Hwy 35 and at the intersection with Hwy 26, keep right, now on Hwy 26, for another 2.2 miles to Government Camp. Turn right (north) onto the Timberline Road, just before the Summit Rest Area. The parking lots for the Lodge are 5.2 miles up the Timberline Road.

Stunted Pine

CLOCKWISE: UMBRELLA FALLS TRAILHEAD TO TIMBERLINE LODGE

If time permits, take a short (¼ mile) side trip to Umbrella Falls through a lush meadow. This will add about 15-30 minutes, allowing time for photos. To do this take the Umbrella Falls Trail (#667) on the *right* (east) side of the Mt Hood Meadows access road. The access to the Timberline Trail is the continuation of the Umbrella Falls Trail (#667), and takes off on the *left* of the Mt Hood Meadows access road almost opposite the short trail to the falls. The trail climbs very gently, passing through beautiful forest and soon coming to open areas where lupines carpet the meadows. There are occasional glimpses of Mt Hood to the north and Mt Jefferson to the south. The stream crossings are particularly colorful with a rich profusion of flowers clustering on the banks. The yellow and pink monkeyflowers are particularly striking. The Umbrella Falls Trail meets the Timberline Trail after 1½ miles.

One of the cairns marking the trail

Turn left onto the Timberline Trail and follow it through exquisite alpine meadows and down into the White River Canyon. Take care crossing the river! Follow the stone cairns to cross the rocky canyon bed and find the continuation of the trail on the far side.

Once on the west side of the canyon, the trail climbs steadily for the rest of the way to Timberline Lodge. First through forest, then through open meadows with the stately and weirdly-shaped dead snags, and finally up along a ridge beside the White River Canyon and across the flank of the mountain to Timberline Lodge.

There are only two places where the Timberline Trail meets another trail: on the climb out of the canyon, less than a mile from the river, where the Timberline Trail and the Pacific Crest Trail (#2000) meet, and closer to Timberline Lodge where there is a short spur trail to the right, to a viewpoint over the White River Canyon.

COUNTERCLOCKWISE: TIMBERLINE LODGE TO UMBRELLA FALLS TRAILHEAD

There are several access trails to the Timberline Trail from Timberline Lodge and the parking lots; all of them take off from the north (mountain) side of the Lodge or the parking areas. Take any of these and turn right onto the combined Pacific Crest Trail (#2000) and Timberline Trail (#600).

The trail soon dips into a shallow gully and continues east going gradually downhill. Continue on the well-marked trail, ignoring a fork to the left that leads to a viewpoint, and continuing to the next fork at 1½ miles from Timberline Lodge. Here the Timberline Trail takes off to the left and the Pacific Crest Trail continues straight, signed to Barlow Pass.

Take the Timberline Trail to the left, and stay on it as it dips down into the White River Canyon, crosses the river, and climbs out on the other side. The trail is well marked by stone cairns and posts as it crosses the wide canyon bed. Crossing the river can be sporting, so look for a suitable crossing place. The trail on the far side of the canyon starts in the draw of trees that dips down to the edge of the canyon, zigzags up for about a mile, flattens out at the treeline and continues through alpine meadows.

Four miles east of Timberline Lodge, the trail crosses a service road leading to Mt Hood Meadows

Ski Area. Just before the service road, the trail forks: the right fork turns acutely back and to the right .

Take the right fork, signed the Umbrella Falls Trail (#667), and follow it down for 1½ miles to the Mt Hood Meadows access road. Umbrella Falls is ¼ mile on the other side of the access road, on the continuation of the Umbrella Falls Trail, and is well worth the extra 15-30 minutes.

PINNACLE RIDGE AND ELK COVE TRAILS

FEATURES: Long alternative access trails to the Timberline Trail from the north, through quiet forest with meadows and alpine flowers. Elk Cove Trail has dramatic views of the north face of Mt. Hood. Pinnacle Ridge Trail has several lovely marshy areas.

DIFFICULTY:
Both trails are Moderately Strenuous
because of the elevation gain

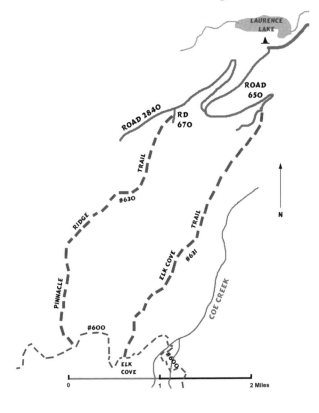

DISTANCES:
Pinnacle Ridge Trail 3.4 miles one way,
Elevation Gain: 2200 ft.

Elk Cove Trail 3.9 miles one way
Elevation Gain: 1900 ft.

MAPS:
Mt. Hood Wilderness Map;
Green Trails: Mt. Hood, #462;
USGS: Mt Hood North

DESCRIPTION: These trails lie between the Vista Ridge Trail and Cloud Cap and provide very attractive alternatives to accessing the Timberline Trail on the north side of the mountain. Both are fairly long access trails, and both climb through forest and meadows.

Marsh Marigold

The Pinnacle Ridge Trail has more open forest and meadows than Vista Ridge and Elk Cove Trails, and is far less used than any of the other access trails. This may be because it has some marshy areas and an uneven grade with flat areas and several steep pitches, so it is hard to keep an even pace. It is fun to try this trail, though, because it is quite different from the other access trails—much less predictable. The marshy areas of the Pinnacle Ridge Trail have some different flowers and grasses from other trails which is an added attraction for the flower lover.

Vine Maple

The Elk Cove Trail is the longest of the access trails (3.9 miles), but the grade is consistently gentle, and there are beautiful meadows and views along the way. Even without the added bonus of the Timberline Trail, this is a lovely hike!

TRAILHEADS:

The trailheads are both accessible from Hwy 35, the Mt Hood Loop Highway.

If taking Hwy 26 east from Portland, pass through Gresham, Sandy, Wemme, Zigzag, Rhododendron and Government Camp. 2.2 miles after Government Camp, at the junction with Hwy 35, take the right fork, now on Hwy 35. Continue north for 17 miles from the junction of Hwys 26 and 35 and turn left (west)

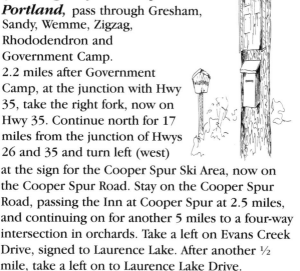

at the sign for the Cooper Spur Ski Area, now on the Cooper Spur Road. Stay on the Cooper Spur Road, passing the Inn at Cooper Spur at 2.5 miles, and continuing on for another 5 miles to a four-way intersection in orchards. Take a left on Evans Creek Drive, signed to Laurence Lake. After another ½ mile, take a left on to Laurence Lake Drive. Laurence Lake is another 4 miles. Continue past the dam to a forest road (2840) on the left signed to Elk Cove Trail and Pinnacle Ridge Trail.

If taking I-84, take the Hwy 35 exit in Hood River. Drive south for 23.5 miles and turn right (west) at the sign for the Cooper Spur Ski Area, now on the Cooper Spur Road. Stay on the Cooper Spur Road, passing the Inn at Cooper Spur at 2.5 miles, and continuing on for another 5 miles to a four-way intersection in orchards. Take a left on Evans Creek Drive, signed to Laurence Lake. After another ½ mile, take a left on to Laurence Lake Drive. Laurence Lake is another 4 miles. Continue past the dam to a forest road on the left signed to Elk Cove Trail and Pinnacle Ridge Trail.

To reach the Pinnacle Ridge Trailhead:

From the Kinnikinnick Campground at Laurence Lake, take Rd 2840 signed to Elk Cove and Pinnacle Ridge Trails. When the road forks at one mile, continue straight, signed to Pinnacle Ridge Trail, for 2.4 miles. The trailhead is on the right just before the road ends, and is marked by a noticeboard and Wilderness Permit Box. The forest road from the Laurence Lake campground has a fairly good gravel surface and passenger cars should have no difficulty.

To reach the Elk Cove Trailhead:

From the Kinnickinnick Campground at Laurence Lake, take Rd 2840 signed to Elk Cove and Pinnacle Ridge Trails. When the road forks at one mile, take the left fork. The last 1.3 miles is rough and narrow in parts, but passable for most passenger cars unless they have very low clearance. The trailhead is on the left, marked by a Wilderness Permit Box.

Remember to sign in at the Wilderness Permit Box.

Avalanche Lily

PINNACLE RIDGE TRAIL

The trail starts out more or less flat through open forest of mostly Douglas Fir, festooned with moss, and heads to the west. It is deceptively easy and flat initially, but soon begins to climb with short steeper pitches interspersed with flatter sections. The trail skirts around to the right of several large outcroppings of rocks and continues to head west for a while, before turning more directly towards Mt Hood.

There are several marshy areas to negotiate and trying to keep your boots dry is futile. Just plunge in and splosh over to dry ground. There are also several exquisite meadows, one very marshy, but all with interesting flowers and grasses, and abundant blueberries. The meadows higher on the trail are much drier and are bordered with heather.

Continue up through several dry gullies, and across narrow streams, to the junction with the Timberline Trail.

Mountain Spirea

ELK COVE TRAIL

The trail takes a couple of switchbacks up to a ridge through an area of forest which is littered with blow down. After the blow down area, the undergrowth is rich with Oregon Grape, ferns, chinquapin, and kinnickinnick. Look also for twin flowers, lupines and beargrass. Further up the trail, dramatic glimpses of Mt Hood appear and there are great views down into the canyon carved by the Coe Branch of the Hood River. The flowers become more plentiful as the trail climbs. There are whole meadows of avalanche lilies. The trail crosses a beautiful stream about 2/3 of the way up, and the forest and undergrowth become more lush. Marsh marigolds cluster in the wet areas and avalanche lilies carpet the forest floor. The trail then takes a few switchbacks before it opens into Elk Cove. There is a good camping area in the forest just before the trail joins the Timberline Trail.

AROUND THE MOUNTAIN
BACKPACKING THE TIMBERLINE TRAIL

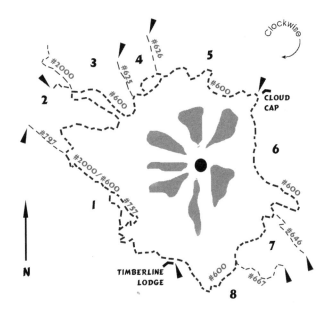

Hiking around Mt. Hood in a single trip provides a different perspective on the mountain than you'll get from encircling the mountain on day hikes. Nothing compares with camping under the stars away from city lights or awakening to the crisp morning air and dew-covered wildflowers. You'll also have the best opportunity to view the full-time residents of the mountain (such as deer, elk, and marmots) if you spend some quiet, uninterrupted time waiting to observe them in the late evening or very early morning. You are unlikely to see the other residents, such as bears, cougars, bobcats and wolverines because there are relatively few of them and they are very shy.

Beginnings
Although you can start at any trailhead mentioned

in this book, the best place to begin a round- the-mountain trip is Timberline Lodge. This will provide you with a good opportunity to check with the rangers on trail conditions and fire danger, get the local weather forecast, recheck your pack for essential gear, and park safely.

Clockwise or Counterclockwise ?

There isn't a "correct" answer to this question. Perhaps the most persuasive consideration is how you want to hike the Timberline Lodge to Ramona Falls segment, which has the largest elevation change. If you hike *clockwise*, this segment is first and, though long (10.2 miles), is mostly downhill. If you hike *counterclockwise*, this segment comes last and is a long uphill haul (3200ft.).

Where can I camp?

Follow "no impact" camping practices. Camping is allowed anywhere in the Wilderness Area but the impact on the fragile alpine environment is minimized by using the areas that are frequently used. Wilderness Area rules prohibit camping within 200 feet of the shoreline of any lake or stream, in the tree-covered islands of Elk Cove and Elk Meadows, within 500 feet of Ramona Falls, or camping in a meadow. Camping etiquette suggests that if you camp outside an established campsite, you should ask other campers whose tents are already set up if camping close by (within 200 feet) is acceptable to them. Respect their quest for a wilderness experience!

How Long Will It Take?

Although a few diehards choose to race the 41-mile Timberline Trail in one day, most choose a more leisurely pace and take 4-5 days. The trip planner below gives some guidance about how to stage your trip if you have 5 days.

Trip Planner for a 5 day trip:

Starting Point	Destination	Distance (miles)
Timberline Lodge	Ramona Falls	10.2
Ramona Falls	Cairn Basin	9.2
Cairn Basin	Cloud Cap Saddle	8.1
Cloud Cap Saddle	Clark Creek	7.1
Clark Creek	Timberline Lodge	6.1

Other Options

To extend your camping trip, you may want to shorten your third day and camp at Dollar Lake (see Segment 5), near Vista Ridge Trail. Although Dollar Lake is only a short distance from Cairn Basin, the lake provides an perfect stopover for an extra night.

Around the Campfire

In keeping with the ethic of "no impact" camping, the Forest Service strongly recommends the use of stoves, not fires, for cooking. However, campfires are permitted in the Mt Hood Wilderness Area, with the exception of the meadows, the tree-covered islands of Elk Cove, Elk Meadows, or within 500 feet of Ramona Falls. Using fire within 500 feet of McNeil Point is also prohibited. If you can't resist the temptation to build a fire, use only downed wood or other dry materials in the area; ***do not*** cut or break off live branches, shrubs or tree limbs; ***never*** build a large fire; and always construct a fire ring around the fire. ***Always*** *douse* the fire with water, *stir* it so that the heat dissipates, and *feel it* to make sure there is no heat left in it. When you break up camp, make sure your fire ring has been pulled part and the rocks and dirt left as naturally as you found them.

Heading for the Woods

The only toilets on the Timberline Trail are in the Cloud Cap campground. Again, in keeping with the "no impact" ethic, toilet tissue should not be left in the woods—even if buried! Take a ziplock bag to carry out used tissue or burn it completely in your campfire. Human waste should be buried in the ground, at least 200 feet from any stream or riverbank. Dig a hole and cover it like a cat. Mother Nature will do the rest of the work if you follow these basic rules of sanitation.

Emergencies

When setting out on a trip, you must be prepared for almost any weather possibility. Emergencies do occur, however, so it is good to know that there are two stone shelters on, or near, the Timberline Trail: one in Cairn Basin (Segment Four) and the other just above the junction of the Cooper Spur Trail #600B and the Tilly Jane Trail #600A (Segment Six). There is also a stone shelter at McNeil Point considerably above the Timberline Trail (Segment Three). Some maps show a shelter in Paradise Park, but this is now ruined. Don't count on having an enjoyable camping experience if you spend a night in one of these stone shelters. They have dirt floors and are small, but they do provide some protection in an emergency. Better than spending the night in a shelter is to be prepared: be sure the gear you take is up to the task of sheltering you from most

any storm. Also, remember that you will pass
trailheads for hikes described in this book. You are
very likely to encounter other hikers (with cars) at
these locations and they may be able to help.

Water
However pristine and tempting it may seem, the
water on Mt Hood is not completely safe and
should never be drunk without treating it with one
of the three methods mentioned in the Introduction
(chemical tabs, filtering, or boiling for 5 minutes).

Weather
For backpackers, preparation for rain takes some
additional planning. Waterproof rain gear—pants
and a jacket, with a hood or a good rain hat— is a
must.

It is also a good idea to take a tarp, some line to
secure the tarp to a tree or bush, and a ground
cloth to go under your tent. These few items weigh
virtually nothing and provide protection in a
downpour. Pack essential gear, such as dry clothing
and sleeping bag, into plastic garbage bags *within
your stuffsack or pack* for extra protection.
Commercial pack covers are available but
expensive. A very large plastic garbage bag or a
fairly inexpensive rain poncho are cheaper
alternatives. Put any of these covers over your pack,
night or day, to keep your gear from getting
drenched.

Hypothermia
Hypothermia is one of the greatest risks when
hiking at high altitude, and the weather doesn't
have to be cold for you to succumb to it. All it takes

is fatigue, wind and your own perspiration to drop your body temperature below its normal limits. Avoid getting chilled and put on a jacket as soon as you stop hiking. Use common sense, be aware of the status of the others in your group, and use the gear you brought.

Animals
There is nothing worse than waking on a crystal clear morning in the mountains to discover that your pack has been torn apart and its contents destroyed during the night by the permanent residents of the mountain. Experienced campers know that they need to string their pack up in a tree or some inaccessible place every night to avoid these surprises. On Mt Hood, it is probably only necessary to get your food (and not your whole pack) out of harm's way. This needn't be difficult if you use the sturdy line or cord you've brought along for this purpose (see equipment list). If you want to get fancy, a carabiner can be used to secure the line to the pack and then thrown over a tall branch of a tree (the 'biner makes the throw easier). Since rodents are the most likely culprit on Mt Hood, you want to let the bag or pack drop as far from the limb as possible. Just let it hang out there by itself and hope it stays that way all night.

Food
A reasonable rule of thumb is to take 1 -1 ½ lbs of food per person per day. Plan every meal in advance and bag meals separately in ziplock bags. Take along plenty of snacks and nibble on them throughout the day. Strenuous hiking trips are NOT the time to go on a diet. Eat at least three meals a day, drink fluids continuously, and snack.

Equipment
It is often said that the backpacker's enjoyment of a trip is inversely related to the weight of their pack.

Don't lug a heavy pack on this hike! On a 41 mile hike, a heavy pack just isn't worth it and isn't necessary; shoot for 25-30 lbs.

To achieve this:
Take only essential gear (listed below) and package it well. Unnecessary wrapping can be removed at home and the contents placed into ziplock bags.

Plan your meals carefully using lightweight, dehydrated food, or minute rice, risotto or other pastas (with envelopes of spaghetti sauce), that are available at the supermarket. Take ziplock bags or paper envelopes with hot or cold cereal for breakfast or snacks. You won't mind a glass of instant milk or Ovaltine if it has been rehydrated with cold mountain stream water (appropriately purified). Granular, sweetened drinks like Kool-Aid or Tang can be added to water (especially if you use purification tablets) for a refreshing change from water during the day.

Don't skimp on warm clothes—even if hot, clear weather is predicted during your hike. Take clothing that is light in volume and weight (e.g., polypro or capalene) and don't forget your hat and light-weight gloves.

What to Take/What not to Take

Footgear

Sturdy boots with ankle support are essential when carrying a backpack. Make sure they have been broken in before the trip. Popular sneaker-style boots may be adequate for day hikes, but this is a serious trip that requires serious footware. Be sure to buy boots from a dealer who knows how to fit them to your feet. The best stores have a tilt board in the shoe department so that you can see if your toes slide forward as you go down an incline. Just in case, pack the moleskin too!

Clothes and Gear

ALL of the following clothing for round -the- mountain:

Boots (waterproofed)
2 pair light weight socks
2 pair medium socks

1 light weight set (top and bottom) of polypro or capalene long underwear
1 pair of wool or poly pants (medium to heavy weight, depending on season)

Rain pants and jacket with hood (or rain hat). Jacket can double as a windbreaker

Brimmed hat or cap with visor
1 long sleeved shirt
1 t-shirt
1 fleece or poly shirt/jacket
1 down or synthetic vest or parka
1 pr light weight poly gloves

Sunglasses
Bandana (the handiest camping item ever invented)
1 wool hat
underwear

Camping Equipment.

The following is a bare-bones list of equipment for a several day backpack:

Ten Essentials (see Introduction)

Water bottle (1 liter)
Back pack fitted to your back (includes hip belt and shoulder pads)
Sleeping bag: stuff first into a plastic garbage bag (compactor bags are best) then into its stuff sack
Foam pad or thinsolite pad/air matress
Tent with a footprint ground cloth or a good plastic ground cloth
Rain fly

Water purification system (filter) or water purification tablets
Cooking pot (If you are travelling very light, take at least one pot)
Pot gripper or thick hot pad
Cup/mug and bowl or plate
Utensils
Waterproof, windproof matches in a case with a striker

Stoves and Fuel.
Do not rely on a campfire for cooking. Cooking with a stove is more efficient and saves precious resources. Buy a good, lightweight version that is fuel efficient and easy to service and repair. Be sure and check your stove and fuel canisters before you leave home. Many a trip has been ruined because the stove malfunctioned or the fuel leaked out of its can.
Stove
Adequate fuel for your trip (2-3 meals per day) PLUS some extra fuel for emergencies and mistakes
Waterproof/windproof matches in a case with a striker that works
Bic lighter

Other Essential Stuff. The following is a list of very important auxilliary equipment for your hike.

Map in a waterproof bag or case
Extra plastic garbage bags (large)
40-50 feet of line or cord
Binoculars
Insect repellent
Sun screen (#15 or better)

Flashlight or headlamp (headlamps are great because they follow you whereever you go plus you can hang them up in your tent once you get inside)
Pocket knife (Leatherman or Swiss Army are ideal)

Chapstick
Toiletries (the bare necessities)
Duct tape (roll a 1-2' supply onto your water bottle or some other piece of equipment)
Your ID
Biodegradable soap (can be purchased at a camping store)

Headnet (if bugs are bad)
1 sml and 1 large bungie
First aid kit (throw in a safety pin and a small mirror if you wear contact lenses)
Additional waterproof/windproof matches and/or extra Bic lighter
This book

Leave at Home on this Trip
You do not need an ice axe.
Resist the temptation to take a cell phone or radio.
There are no places to fish, so leave the fishing line at home.

Mile	Timberline Trail #600	Mile
0	Timberline Lodge.	40.7
1	Wilderness Boundary	39.7
1.1	Cross Little Zigzag Canyon	39.6
1.4	Jct. Hidden LK. Tr.#779	39.3
2.2	Viewpoint Zigzag Canyon and Mississippi Head	38.5
3.3	Cross Zigzag River	37.4
3.7	S. Jct. Paradise Loop Tr.#757.	37
4.2	Jct. Paradise Park Tr.#778	36.5
5	Cross Lost Creek - view of falls	35.7
5.6	Cross Rushing Water Creek	35.1
6.1	N. Jct. Paradise Loop Tr.	34.6
7.4	View of Slide Mt., Rushing Water Creek	33.3
9.4	Sandy River Crossing. Cairns mark trail.	31.3
9.7	Jct. Ramona Falls loop Tr.797	31
10.2	Ramona Falls. Camping restrictions	30.5
10.9	Jct. Yocum Ridge Tr.#771	29.8
13.3	Muddy Fork - 2 crossings.	27.4
15.5	Wilderness Boundary	25.2
15.7	Jct. Pacific Crest Trail w/ Timberline Trail	25
16.3	Jct. McGee Creek Tr.#627	24.4
16.7	Wilderness Boundary	24
18.3	Cross McGee Creek	22.4
18.7	Jct. Mazama Trail #625.	22
19.4	Cairn Basin (stone shelter).	21.3
20.6	Eden Park	20.8
20.8	Cross Ladd Creek	20.6
20.9	Jct. Vista Ridge Tr.#626	19.9
21.2	Wy'east Basin (jct upper trail from Cairn Basin)	19.5
21.7	Jct. Pinnacle Ridge Tr.#630	19.2
22.7	Jct. Elk Cove Tr.#631 Camping restrictions	18
23.6	Cross Coe Creek	17.1
25.5	Cross branch of Compass Creek	15.2
27.2	Cross Eliot Branch	13.5
27.5	Cloud Cap Saddle (campground) Water/pit toilet.	13.2
27.7	Wilderness Boundary	13
28.6	Jct. Tilly Jane Tr.#600A & Cooper Spur Tr.#600B.	12.1
29.8	Cross Lambertson Spur (7320 feet)	10.9
31.1	Gnarl Ridge	9.6
32.3	Jct. Gnarl Ridge Tr.#652 (Elk Meadows 1 mile east)	8.4
33.1	Cross Newton Creek - unbridged	7.6
33.7	Jct. Newton Creek Trail #646	7
34.1	Wilderness Boundary	6.6
34.6	Cross Clark Creek unbridged	6.1
37	Cross Mitchell Creek. Jct. Umbrella Falls Tr.#667	3.7
38.3	Cross White River. (in high water cross upstream)	2.4
39.4	Jct. Pacific Crest Trail. North PCT &Timberline Trail	1.3
40.3	Cross headwaters of Salmon River	0.4
40.7	Timberline Lodge.	0

BUSINESS RESOURCES IN THE MT HOOD AREA

LODGINGS

NORTH(close to I-84)

Cascade Locks (zip code OR 97041)

Bridge of the Gods Motel & RV Park   (541) 374-8628

630 WaNaPa St., **Cascade Locks,**

Motel with mini kitchens & RV Park with full hook-ups, cable TV, 8:00am-11:00pm

Hood River (zip code OR 97031)

The Roomfinder operated by the Hood River Bed & Breakfast Association is a free lodging locator service representing over 10 local lodging providers   (541)386-6767

4079 Barrett Drive

Best Western Hood River Inn   (541) 386-2200

1108 E. Marina Way   Fax   (541) 386-8905

Accommodations, restaurant, banquets, catering. 149 rooms; on shore of Columbia River with mountain views, heated swimming pool, private beach.

Brown's Bed & Breakfast   (541) 386-1545

3000 Read Road

Farmhouse B&B built in the 1930's and remodeled in 1995. Two bedrooms, one with mountain, one with orchard view. Farm breakfast.

Cascade Avenue Bed & Breakfast   (541) 387-2377

823 Cascade Ave   Fax   (541) 387-3114

Quaint English cottage in downtown Hood River. Two air-conditioned rooms with river view.

Columbia Gorge Hotel   (541) 386-5566

4000 Westcliff Drive   Fax (541) 387-5414

Restored historic inn on 11 acres, atop 210 ft waterfall. Restaurant with award-winning cuisine.

Cottonwood   (541) 387-5550

204 13th St

One bedroom kitchen units close to downtown Hood River. Weekly rentals or B&B on weekends.

Hood River Hotel   (800) 386-1859   (541) 386-1900

102 Oak Ave   Fax (541)-386-6090

National Historic landmark; river view rooms and kitchen suites; jacuzzi, sauna & exercise facility; and banquet rooms. email: HRHotel@gorge.net

Hood River Vacation Rentals   (541) 387-3113
823 Cascade Ave   Fax (541) 387-3114
Specializing in vacation rentals. Accommodations include
Rowena Riverfront Homes, Hood River Cottages, Condos,
and Bed and Breakfast.

Lakecliff Estate Bed & Breakfast   (541) 386-7000
3820 Westcliff Drive   Fax (541) 386-1803
Historic home on cliff above the Columbia River; large rooms
with fireplaces; views. May through Labor Day.

Love's Riverview Lodge   (800) 789-9568 (541) 386-8719
1505 Oak St   Fax (541) 386-6671
Motel with refrigerators, microwaves, in-room coffee, HBO.
Pool & spa planned for summer 1997

The Beryl House Bed & Breakfast   (541)386-5567
4079 Barrett Drive
Farmhouse set in the orchards of the Hood River Valley.

Mt Hood, Parkdale (zip code OR 97041)

Inn at Cooper Spur   (541) 352-6692
10755 Cooper Spur Road, Mt Hood   Fax (541) 352-7551
Accommodations and restaurant; log cabin rentals and motel
units in wilderness setting with views of Mt Hood, Mt Adams
& Mt Rainier

Mt Hood Bed & Breakfast   (541) 352-6885
8885 Cooper Spur Rd, Parkdale   (800) 557-8885
Small working ranch and B&B on 42 acres on the shoulder of
Mt Hood. Four guest rooms with VCRs. Views of Mt Hood,
Mt Adams & Mt Rainier. Indoor tennis, sauna & outdoor spa.

Mt Hood Hamlet Bed & Breakfast   (541) 352-3574
6741 Highway 35, Mt Hood   (800) 407-0570
New B&B with three guest rooms. Views of Mt Hood

The Dalles (zip code OR 97058)

Days Inn   (800) 991-0801 (541) 296-1191
2500 W 6th St   Fax (541) 298-2455
Hotel with free continental breakfast, outdoor pool & spa

Troutdale (zip code 97060)

McMenamins Edgefield   (800) 669-8610 (503) 669-8610
2126 SW Halsey   Fax (503)665-4209
European-style village on the site of the historic Multnomah
County Poor Farm built in 1911. restaurant, winery, brewery,
movie theater, banquet facility, pub.

LODGINGS

SOUTH OF THE MOUNTAIN

Government Camp (Zip Code 97028)

Falcon's Crest Inn   (800) 624-7384 (503)272-3403
87287 Gov't Camp Loop   Fax (503) 272-3454
Lodging, bed & breakfast, dining, conference center, private
and mystery parties. Small groups welcome. Christmas
holiday specialists, 6 a.m.-11:00 p.m. daily.

Golden Poles Chalet   (503) 272-3337
P.O. Box 399
Condos; 4 units rented by owners. Swimming pool, sauna.

Huckleberry Inn   (503) 272-3325
Gov't Camp Loop
Standard, deluxe and bunk rooms.

Mt. Hood Inn   (503) 272-3307   Res. 1-800-443-7777
87450 E. Gov't Camp Loop
56 rooms, in-room spas, continental breakfast, guest laundry,
ski lockers and wax room.

Mt. Hood Manor   (503) 272-3440
88900 Gov't Camp Loop   (800) 514-3400
Four spacious rooms with private bath, family-style breakfast,
TV/VCR's, outdoor hot tub.

Summit Meadows Cabins   ph/fax (503) 272-3494
P.O. Box 235
Vacation rentals, cabins and homes for 2-12. Two miles south
of Government Camp. Wooded creek-side setting beside
Summit Meadow; miles of trails. Res. recommended.
9:00am—9:00 pm., message phone.

Thunderhead Lodge   (503) 272-3368
87577 Gov't Camp Loop   (800) 859-8493
Privately-owned condos with full-size kitchens; sleep 2-10.
Heated swimming pool, rec room with ping-pong/foos ball,
pool table, storage area for skis/bikes.

Timberline Lodge   (503) 272-3311   Res: (800) 547-1406
A National Historic Landmark with ski area (winter and
summer skiing),hotel with 70 guest rooms and award-winning
cuisine, gift shop and food service.

Trillium Lake Basin Cabins   (503)272-0151
P.O. Box 28
Cabins on Mineral Creek with view of Mt. Hood peak;
adjacent to Multorpor Mtn and the Barlow Trail.

View House   (503) 272-3295
P.O. Box 133
Weekend rental cabin, fully equipped, sleeps 6-8.

Zigzag, Rhododendron, Welches, Wemme, Brightwood
(zip codes, Zigzag, Rhododendron, OR 97049;
Wemme, Welches, OR 97067; Brightwood, OR 97011)

The Brightwood Guest House B&B   (503) 622-5783
64725 E Barlow Trail Road (P.O.Box 330), Brightwood
Fully-equipped cabin, oriental design, deck, gourmet
breakfast, bikes

Cascade Property Management   (503) 622-5688
24403 E. Welches Road, Suite 104, Welches
Cabins, cottages, homes and contemporary condos close to
skiing, hiking golfing, biking and fishing. All homes fully
furnished. 9:00a.m-6:00 p.m., Mon.-Fri; 10:00am-5:00pm,
Sat; 11.00am-5.00pm on Sun

Cedar Grove Cottage   (503) 557-8292
23782 E. Sampson Ave., Welches
Contact address: 28350 SW Mountain Road, West Linn 97068
Fully equipped cottage with fireplace and spa on secluded,
forested acre in Welches

Doublegate Inn Bed & Breakfast   (503) 622-4859
26711 E. Welches Road, Welches
Three "storybook" guest rooms, private baths with spa or
soak tub. Full breakfast incl. "will make your tummy smile"

The Resort at The Mountain   (503) 622-3101
68010 East Fairway Ave., Welches   (800) 669-7666
100- year old resort in 300 acres: 160 guest rooms and suites;
27-hole golf course; tennis courts; outdoor heated pool and
jacuzzi; fitness center; bike rentals; golf lessons; volleyball;
croquet; lawn bowling. Full conference/banquet facilities

.

RESTAURANTS

NORTH OF THE MOUNTAIN

Cascade Locks

Charburger   (541) 374-8477
745 WaNaPa
Charburgers, seafood, steaks, chili, soups, 6:00am-9:00pm

East Wind Drive-In   (541) 374-8380
395 Wanapa St
10am-9pm. Burgers, fries, shakes, ice cream, espresso

Hood River

Bette's Place Restaurant   (541) 386-1880
416 Oak St
Breakfast & lunch: M-F 5.30am-5pm; Sat/Sun 5.30am-4pm.
Home-made soups, cinnamon rolls, vegetarian food, omelets

Carolyn's Restaurant   (541) 386-1127
1313 Oak St
Breakfast & lunch in family restaurant with Columbia River
view, 6:00am-2:00pm daily

Pasquale's Ristorante   (541) 386-1900
102 Oak Ave
In the Hood River Hotel, a national historic landmark. Italian
& Northwest cuisine, 7:00am-9:00pm

Santacroce's Italian Restaurant   (541) 354-2511
4780 Hwy 35
W-Sat 4:00-11:00pm; Sun 2-10pm. Pizzas, entrees & salads

The Mesquitery Restaurant and Bar   (541) 386-2002
1219 12th St.
Lunch W-F 11.30-2:00pm; Dinner 7 nights at 4.30pm.
Mesquite grill steaks, seafood, pasta, ribs, chicken, salads

RESTAURANTS
SOUTH OF THE MOUNTAIN
Government Camp/Timberline Lodge

Charlie's Mountain View   (503)272-3333
88462 Gov't Camp Loop
Full service restaurant. Live music/karaoke, 11.30am-2.30am.

Huckleberry Inn   (503) 272-3325
Gov't Camp Loop
Breakfast, lunch and dinner.

Mt. Hood Brew Pub   (503) 272-3724
87304 E. Gov't Camp Loop
Fresh ales and stout from Mt. Hood Brewing Co.; pizzas,
sandwiches, salads, espresso. 12:00 - 10:00 pm Sun.- Thurs,
12:00-11:00pm. Fri. and Sat.

Timberline Lodge   (503) 272-3311
Award-winning restaurants in Lodge; snack bar and bar in
Day Lodge.

Zigzag, Rhododendron
Alpine Hut Restaurant   503) 622-4618
73365 E. Hwy. 26, Rhododendron
Breakfast, lunch, dinner and cocktails in a mountain
atmosphere, 7:00am-10:00pm.

Barlow Trail Inn   (503) 622-3112
69580 E. Hwy. 26, Zigzag
Breakfast, lunch, dinner, full lounge, large covered deck, air
conditioned. Historic log building.

Don Guidos Italian Cuisine   (503) 622-5141
73330 E. Hwy. 26, Rhododendron
In historic Log Lodge at base of Mt. Hood. Opens at 5:00pm.

Old Oregon Trail Restaurant   (503) 622-3775
71545 E. Hwy 26, Rhododendron
Home-style cooking in restaurant with spectacular
chandeliers

Zigzag Inn   (503) 622-4779
70162 E. Hwy. 26, Zigzag
Casual restaurant and lounge in historic log building. Pizza,
pasta, burgers, steak, chicken, vegetarian dishes, milk shakes.

Welches/Wemme/Brightwood

Honey Bear Express   (503) 622-5726
Hoodland Plaza, Hwy. 26 & Welches Road, Welches
Deli sandwiches, daily specials and soups, espresso, ice cream
and candy. Take-out. 9:00am-5:00pm daily

Inn-Between Restaurant/Lounge
67858 E. Hwy. 26, Welches
Full-service menu, "cook your own steaks," many draft and
micro-beers, live music Fri/Sat.

Chalet Swiss Specialty Restaurant   (503) 622-3600
Hwy. 26 at Welches Road, Welches
A Mt. Hood dining tradition for 22 years, featuring Swiss and
northwest cuisine. 5:00 p.m. Wed.-Sun.

Courtyard Cafe & Catering   (503) 622-5222
65000 East Hwy. 26, Brightwood
Breakfast, lunch, espresso, vegetarian specials, homemade
pastries; catering and banquets.

Mt. Hood Coffee Roasters and Mercantile   (503) 622-5153
64235 E. Brightwood Loop Road, Brightwood
Coffee beans roasted on site, fresh roasted hazelnuts, espresso
drinks and sodas, Dolce syrups, coffee-related merchandise,
local artists' displays. Summer: Wed-Sun 9:00 a.m.-6:00 p.m
Watch for tourist information signs or call for directions.

The Resort at The Mountain   (503) 622-3101
68010 East Fairway Ave., Welches
Highlands Restaurant featuring northwest cuisine and
selections with a Scottish flavor. Open for breakfast, lunch
and dinner; special Sunday brunch. Tartans Inn & Pub by the
golf course offers breakfast, lunch or snack

Espresso Deli   (503) 668-9477
38753 Proctor Blvd, Sandy
Bagels, soups, sandwiches, box lunches
Mountain Moka   503) 668-6811
17450 Meinig Ave, Sandy
Espresso, (also featuring organic espresso), Italian sodas,
bagels, pastries, soft serve frozen yoghurt, shakes, specialty
blended drinks, reading area, espresso. Mon-Fri. 6:00am-7:00
pm, Sat-Sun 7:00a.m-7:00p.m.

MARKETS, WINE, GIFTS, ESPRESSO, BOOKSTORES

NORTH OF THE MOUNTAIN

Cascade Locks
Charburger Gift Shop   (541) 374-8477
745 WaNaPa
Columbia Market   (541) 374-8425
450 WaNaPa
Espresso, 24-hr film processing, meat, produce, ice, firewood

Hood River
Full Sail Brewing Company   (541) 386-2281
506 Columbia St.
Brewery tours available. Light snacks. Summer 12-8pm daily
Ikote' Gifts   (541) 387-3786
202 Cascade Ave.
10am-6pm. Jewelry, full-on bead store, percussion
instruments, candles & incense, patches, scarves, Ecuadorian
imports
The Gift House   (541) 386-9234
204 Oak Avenue
Oregon & Northwest souvenirs, T-shirts, gourmet jams &
foods; wines 9:00am-6:30pm.
The Wine Sellers   (541) 386-4647
514 State St.
Domestic & imported wines, fresh french bread, specialty
foods, chocolates, espresso & gifts
9.30am-5.30pm Mon-Fri; 9.30am-5pm Sat
Waucoma Bookstore   (541) 386-5353
212 Oak St.
9.30am-6.30pm Mon-Fri; 9.30-6 Sat; Sun (summer) 12-4pm.
Coffee beans, pottery, music

Mt Hood
Floral-N-Hardies   (541) 352-6662
6550 Cooper Spur Rd., Mt Hood
Gifts, Oregon jams & foods, local artists' work, dinnerware,
lamps, books, frames, quilts, candles, ornaments, fresh
flowers, Tue-Sat 10:30-5:30; Sun-Mon Summer
Mt Hood Country Store & Deli   (541) 352-6024
6545 Cooper Spur Rd, Mt Hood
Full service grocery, home-made foods, deli, espresso,
sandwiches, baked desserts, micro brews, NW wines, antiques
& collectibles. Mon-Sat 8am-7.30pm, Sun 8-6.30; drive-up
coffee window open at 7am

The Dalles
Klindts Booksellers   (541) 296-3355
315 E. 2nd St
Historic bookstore, new & used hardbacks, gift items,
stationery, coffee, soft drinks 9:00-5:30 Mon-Sat, 11-4 Sun

SOUTH OF THE MOUNTAIN
Alpine Sports/Shirt Shop   (503)668-4023
38821 Proctor Blvd., Sandy
Bike sales & rentals, T-shirts, some sports equipment
Mountain Sports   (503) 622-4736
Hoodland Plaza, Welches
Active wear for all seasons, accessories
Trillium Gift Shop, Resort at The Mountain (503) 622-3101
68010 East Fairway Ave, Welches
Local crafts, gifts

Shaggy Mane Mushroom

THINGS TO DO
NORTH OF THE MOUNTAIN

Cascade Locks (zipcode 97014)
Mountain Shadow Ranch   (541) 374-8592
H.C. 66, Box 690   *Email: fox@gorge.net*
Guided horseback rides for all ages in the Columbia River
Scenic Area. Res. recommended

Hood River (zipcode 97031)
 Big Winds   (541) 386-6086
505 Cascade   Fax (541) 386-3713
Windsurfing retail /rental shop with rentals & lessons
White Salmon (zipcode 98672)
Phil's White Water Adventures   (509) 493-2641
38 Northwestern Lake
Guided raft trips on the White Salmon, April-Sept

THINGS TO DO
SOUTH OF THE MOUNTAIN
Government Camp (zipcode 97208)
The Art of Adventure Raft Trips   (503) 272-0120
P.O. Box 250
Mt. Hood Brewing Company   (503) 272-0102
87304 E. Gov't Camp Loop
Individual & group tours at the Brew Pub adjacent to brewery.
Mt. Hood Ski Bowl Winter & Summer Res. (503)272-3206
P.O. Box 280   Ptld: 222-2695
>20 attractions in summer incl, Alpine slide, mountain
biking, horseback riding, bungee jumping, go-carts. Mon.-Fri.
11:00a.m.-6:00p.m. Weekends & Holidays: 10:00 a.m.-7:p.m.
Timberline Ski Area (zipcode 97028)
Timberline   (503) 272-3311
Winter and summer skiing

GAS, TOWING, AND FOOD MARTS
SOUTH OF THE MOUNTAIN (only)

Alpine Towing, Rhododendron   (503) 622-3365
 24-hr towing

Chevron Food Mart, Wapinitia Meadows   (503) 622-3017
Ice, hot deli, espresso, big selection of camping and fishing
supplies; fishing licenses, boat passes, Warm Springs fishing
permits, tire chains, snow park permits. Summer: 7.00am-
8:00pm, Mon-Thurs, 7.00am-9pm, Fri-Sun.

Janz Berryland   (503) 668-7415
41777 Hwy. 26, **Sandy**
Wholesale & retail produce, local crafts, plants.

Mt. Hood Foods   (503) 622-4652
73265 E. Hwy. 26 **Rhododendron**
General merchandise, groceries, deli, videos, fishing supplies,
sporting goods.

Purdy's Towing   (503) 622-3153
64025 E. Brightwood Loop Rd. **Brightwood**
Lockout, jump start, gas and towing, 24-hr service.

Shorty's Corner   (503) 668-4144
42600 SE Hwy. 26, **Sandy**
Gas, cafe, groceries

Summit Chevron   (503)272-3692
90140 E. Gov't Camp Loop. **Government Camp**
Hot deli, espresso, tire chains, snow park permits, beer, wine,
pop, ice, worms, camping and fishing supplies. 7:00 a.m.-8:00
p.m. daily.

Zigzag Mountain Store
Hwy. 26 **Zigzag**
General merchandise, gas.

Chanterelle Mushroom

INFORMATION

Mt Hood Visitors Information Center
65000 E. Hwy 26
Welches, OR 97067
(503) 622-4822

Mt Hood Area Chamber of Commerce
PO Box 819
65000 E. Hwy 26
Welches, OR 97067
(503) 622-3017

Hood River County Chamber of Commerce
Port Marina Park
Hood River, OR 97031
(541) 386-2000 or (800) 366-3530

Sandy Area Chamber of Commerce
PO Box 536
39250 Pioneer Street
Sandy, OR 97055
(503) 668-4006

Columbia River Gorge NSA
902 Wasco Avenue, Suite 200
Hood River, OR 97031
(541) 386-2333

US Forest Service
Hood River Ranger Station
6730 Hwy 35
Parkdale, OR 97041
(541) 352-6002

US Forest Service
Zig Zag Ranger Station
70220 E. Hwy 26
Zig Zag, OR 97049
(503) 622-3191